£15

MANORIAL RECORDS

MANORIAL RECORDS

An introduction to their transcription and translation

Denis Stuart

Phillimore

1992

Published by
PHILLIMORE & CO. LTD.
Shopwyke Hall, Chichester, Sussex

ISBN 0 85033 821 2

Printed by Chichester Press Limited

Contents

Acknowledgements

My grateful thanks to Jo-Ann Buck, Dudley Fowkes, Douglas Johnson and Barbara Stuart for comments, criticisms and help in many ways, and Tony Rogers who did the basic photography. I am also grateful to Christine Hanson and Phillimore for the suggestions on content and editing of a difficult text. For the patience and participation which helped me to evolve the method of teaching used in this book special thanks must go to a whole generation of students in my Latin and palaeography classes at the Department of Adult and Continuing Education, University of Keele. Permission to reproduce the longer extracts from documents used in this book has kindly been granted as follows: the Marquess of Anglesey and the Staffordshire Record Office for Example 7 D(W)1734/2/1/491-520; example 11, 15, 19, 20, 25 D(W)1734/2/1; example 22, 30 D(W)1734/2/3/112a; example 24 D(W)1734/2/3/1; the Staffordshire Record Office for example 5 (a) (b) (c) D(W)1522-33; example 6, 10, 17, 18 D(W)0/3/1202; the Public Record Office for example 26, Exch. E 106/2/2; the Controller, HMSO for example 13 DL 30 (Crown Copyright); Keele University Librarian for example 12, Sneyd. mss; The Provost and Scholars of King's College, Cambridge and Cambridge University Librarian for example 31, Kings BEC/26 (Dd.33)

Introduction:
Aims and Methods

This is a 'do-it-yourself' manual intended for students of local history who wish to research on medieval and early modern manorial records. It assumes that the student already has a basic, even if imperfect knowledge of Latin, and some ability to read the older forms of handwriting in English. This book seeks to help such persons to acquire further skill to transcribe and translate manorial records. The approach is graduated, starting with explanations of the nature of the different types of manorial record, and proceeding through a study of the vocabulary of such records and the abbreviations which are encountered to examples of manuscript entries in actual manorial documents. Practice is provided at each stage, with representative extracts from records of the 13th to the 18th centuries. 'Exercises' refer to extracts from documents already fully or partly transcribed; 'Examples' refer to extracts from documents reproduced in their original manuscript form. Most entries are followed by palaeographical, grammatical and other explanatory notes, and extra help with palaeography and abbreviations is in an appendix. Answers to the exercises and examples are provided at the end of the book, together with a dictionary of all words and phrases found in the extracts, and lists of declensions and conjugations.

Latin is a logical, structured language and once an accurate transcription of a document has been made, the correct translation is a matter of the application of the principles of accidence and syntax. Contrary to popular belief the scribes who compiled manorial records were not usually poor Latinists, although medieval business Latin is very free from the point of view of classical grammatical usage. Moreover, most manorial records are written in a set form with standard forms of expression and terminology continually repeated. Once the technical vocabulary has been understood and the abbreviations mastered, both transcription and translation are largely a matter of experience, practice and perseverance. The beginner should not expect to get every word and meaning immediately or pick up a document and read it as easily as does a practised scholar. Where a problem is experienced the difficulty can usually be overcome by going on with the transcription and translation in the expectation that the repetition of a word or phrase will solve the problem. The help of a professional Latin scholar will still sometimes be needed for the elucidation of a difficult word but such persons should not be asked to undertake lengthy transcriptions. Finally, do not assume that a knowledge of grammar is unnecessary: the more grammar you have the greater will be your ability to handle medieval records.

For the student who has his own documents to translate, other works of reference will be necessary. Eileen Gooder's glossary in *Latin for Local History* (Longmans, 2nd edition, 1978) provides a first easy reference for most of the medieval local history vocabulary. The serious research student should also have ready access to R. E. Latham, *Revised Medieval Latin Word-List* (O.U.P., 1965), the standard authority, which also provides numerous variant spellings. P. D. A. Harvey (ed.) *Manorial Records of Cuxham, Oxfordshire, c.1200-1359* (Hist, Mss. Comm. Joint Publication 23, Oxfordshire Records Society, 1, 1976) contains a glossary of words not found in Latham.

Most medieval manorial records are written in what is rather misleadingly called 'Court Hand', i.e. a cursive or semi-cursive script used for its speed and thus differing from the ceremonious hand of charters, etc. and from the idiosyncratic hands employed by government departments. By the 16th century 'Secretary Hand' was developing, and there

are a few examples of this among the extracts in this book. There are numerous printed
alphabets available to help the beginner, one of the most useful of which is in Wright's *Court
Hand Restored* (5th edition, 1818). A reproduction of this is in the appendix. Examples of
single, separate letters, however, are not always completely satisfactory aids to transcription
and in practice it is often better to attempt to read whole words and phrases. There is no
harm in guessing, once you have an idea of what is to be expected, provided you carefully
check. For further help with palaeography, among the many primers available the following
are recommended: F. G. Emmison, *How to Read Local Archives 1500-1700* (Historical
Association, 1967, and numerous reprints); H. E. P. Grieve, *Examples of English Handwriting*
(Essex Record Office Publication No. 21. 5th impression, 1981); L. C. Hector, *The
Handwriting of English Documents* (Kohler and Coombes, facsimile edition 1976); K. C.
Newton, *Medieval Local Records: A Reading Aid* (Historical Association, 1971); C. T. Martin, *The
Record Interpreter* (Phillimore, 1982), and A. Cappelli, *Dizionario di Abbreviature latine ed italiane*
(U. Hoepli, Milan, 6th edition, 1929 and further impressions).

A good classical Latin dictionary and a text-book of Latin grammar are also necessary.
Although the sense and essentials of a document may be obtained readily enough by a
beginner, complete and correct transcriptions and translations do need a knowledge of
classical Latin. For this purpose B. H. Kennedy, *The Revised Latin Primer* (edited by
J. Mountford, Longmans, 1986) is concise and authoritative. (Note that Gooder, *op. cit.*,
refers to Kennedy's *Shorter Latin Primer*, which has a different pagination).

A thorough general knowledge of the topic of the medieval manor and its records is
necessary if the student is to undertake research using material of this nature. The first
chapter of this book provides a sufficient introduction for the beginner to undertake
autonomous research and further reference may be made to the following: P. D. A. Harvey,
Manorial Records (British Records Association, Archives and the User No. 5, 1984); N. Hone
The Manor and Manorial Records (Methuen, 1906), F. G. Emmison, *Elizabethan Life: Home, Work
and Land, Part 3* (Essex County Council, 1976).

Chapter 1:
The Manor and Manor Court Procedure

Introduction

The following summary of the nature of the manor, manor courts and manor court procedure necessarily simplifies a complex system which had many local variations. The origins of the manor are uncertain, but by the time of Domesday Book the manorial system was established throughout most of the country. The manor system may be described as a territorial unit originally held by feudal tenure – held by a landlord, not necessarily titled, who himself was a tenant of the Crown or of a mesne lord who held land directly of the Crown. The manor had a number of aspects. In the medieval period it was an economic unit, usually consisting of the demesne which the lord retained for his own use, and the remainder which was tenanted or used for common or waste. The two main types of tenant were villeins who occupied their lands on condition of rendering services to the lord, such as cultivating his demesne, and freemen who paid a money rent, generally a fixed sum, to the lord. Often individuals occupied lands on both kinds of tenure, and the history of the manor in one respect is the story of the decay of the system of labour services and the evolution of tenures based wholly on money rents. Villein tenure thus evolved into copyhold tenure, that is, the tenant's title was written on the manor court rolls, of which he had a copy – hence the name. All conveyances of copyhold land had to pass through the lord's manorial court where his financial interests were preserved by the imposition of an entry fine in the case of a new tenant and a heriot, or best beast, usually a money payment, in the case of an heir to a deceased tenant. Copyhold tenure was abolished in 1922. Other types of tenant included tenants-at-will and tenants of demesne, and these usually had less security of tenure than freeholders or copyholders.

By right a lord of the manor could hold a court for his local tenants. This was the court baron, usually held every three weeks. Its general business was to state the customs of the manor, whether relating to land tenure or land use, and enforce payment of all dues and performance of all services owed by the tenants to the lord. The court had other powers as well, and was in practice an organ of local government with legislative, administrative and judicial functions. It also had jurisdiction over disputes between individuals and over personal actions by tenants, such as the recovery of small debts and complaints of trespass. The court appointed some local officials, including the reeve or bailiff, who collected the lord's dues, and the hayward.

Many manorial lords also had the right to hold a court leet, usually held every six months. This court inspected the working of the frankpledge, a system of mutual responsibility within a group of about ten households for the maintenance of law and order, and which was often called the view of frankpledge. It had powers to deal with offences such as common nuisances, affrays and the breaking of the assize of bread and ale, and could fine and imprison offenders. Some local officers, including the constable, were appointed at this court. In practice the functions of the court baron and court leet were not necessarily kept distinct. Geographically the manor was sometimes co-terminous with the parish; there might be more than one manor within the parish boundaries, and many manors overlapped from one parish into the next. The venue of a manor court, for example the hall of the lord's house or even the open air at some local site, was prescribed by custom. If the lord was an ecclesiastic the court was usually held in one of the episcopal or conventual buildings.

Sometimes the lord of a small manor himself presided over the manor court, but more often, and especially for the larger manors, this function was performed by the lord's steward or by his deputy. The tenants who attended the manor court were known collectively as the 'homage'(a term which also means the ceremonial act of obligation made by a tenant to the lord, followed by the oath of fealty). Free tenants were in many manors required in principle to attend every court baron but in others the obligation was only for a very few attendances in the year. All villeins by reason of their servile status owed common suit of court, so were obliged to attend. Persons who failed to attend at three consecutive courts, or did not provide an essoin, in effect an excuse with some person nominated by the absentee to stand proxy, were fined.

Manor court procedure varied locally and the following may be taken only as a general account of a court leet fused with a court baron. More detailed discussion of particular points may be found later in this book, and in the other works listed earlier. In a large manor or group of manors the steward summoned the court by precept or message to the local bailiffs, who fixed a notice to the church door or had it read out in church. The court was opened and closed with a formal proclamation, jurors answered to their names, which are sometimes recorded in the roll, and swore, usually four at a time, to make a true presentment. The steward then charged them formally with the articles of the inquest (the points about which the court had to inquire). These included such questions as whether every male over 12 years old was enrolled in tithing or frankpledge, whether all suitors were present or had sent their essoins and whether any offences against the custom of the manor, or other sorts of offences, had been committed. The chief pledges or head tithingmen of each vill within the manor made their presentments of absentees and of offenders, while the court noted any surrenders or transfers or other transactions involving land in which the lord was financially concerned. New tenants, if any, were formally admitted on the payment of the customary fees or fines, with due performance of the usual manorial ceremonies, and then swore an oath of fealty to the lord. The court heard the pleas of litigants, complaints of trespass, assault, unpaid debts, and so on, and decided whether an offender or a litigant was 'in mercy'. The actual amount of any amercement or fine was left to the decision of affeerers (assessors), at the end of the court's proceedings.

Manorial juries had developed by the end of the 13th century, taking over the function that had formerly belonged to the entire body of suitors. In some manor court rolls the jury as a whole made the presentments. They delivered judgment on pleas brought by individuals, and in the medieval period often based these decisions on the principle of compurgation, that is witnesses to the character and truthfulness of the litigant. Sometimes the names of jurors are listed in the court roll, bracketed by the word *jurati* (sworn). The number could vary, though for a court leet the roll sometimes contains the words 'the twelve for the king' or some similar phrase.

Court rolls, the record of the manor courts, became fuller and more formalised by the later medieval period. They may exist as drafts, sometimes called court papers, or as fair copies written afterwards. Officially, up to 1733, with the exception of the period of the Commonwealth, they were written in Latin, but the actual manor court proceedings were conducted in English. Presumably the scribe made a hasty record in Latin, hence the need for the use of abbreviations and common form phrases, standard verbal formulae. Occasionally it is evident that some of the court roll had been written out beforehand, leaving only names and amounts of fines to be inserted.

The agricultural routine of the manor was collectively regulated at the manor court. The detailed orders concerning crop rotation, fallowing, dates of opening and closing the open fields to common pasture, are seldom recorded in the manor court rolls, which were concerned mainly with those matters which directly involved the lord's financial interests. Much of the seasonal routine, however, may be deduced from the presentments of offenders against the routine. Not infrequently later rolls contain orders concerning the running of the open field system, sometimes called 'pains laid', which were penalties laid down for infraction of the rules.

The Latin Vocabulary of Manor Court Rolls
The earliest surviving manor court roll in this country dates from 1246, but by the 1270s such documents were abundant. From the outset most manor courts conducted a variety of business, and the distinctions made between types of court by later legal theorists did not always obtain. By the later 13th century the two main types of court were being recorded, the court baron [*curia baronis/ baronum/ prima/ customaria*] and the court leet or view of frankpledge [*curia leta, visus franciplegii*]. The terms small court and great court [*curia parva/ magna*] are sometimes used as alternatives to court baron and court leet. Other types of court included the court of survey and recognition, the court of pannage, the court of pie powder, and the woodmote or forest court. Only the court baron and view of frankpledge are dealt with in this book as being the most commonly found and most useful for general local history research purposes.

The court baron was the court of the chief tenants of the manor and most often included the business of the court customary of the bond or villein tenants. It was normally held every three weeks, the steward [*senescallus*] presiding. It was attended by all those free tenants who owed 'suit of court' [*secta/ de communi secta/ de communi/ debet sectam curie*], and whose attendance at the court was one of the conditions of their occupation of a tenement, and by the unfree tenants [*villani*] who occupied lands within the manor on a servile tenure [*terre villani*], thus being required to perform weekly and seasonal services on the lord's demesne. In theory all adult males attended, the definition of adult varying but usually taken to be those over 12 years of age. Probably in practice only manorial officers, offenders, jurymen, witnesses, litigants and pledges came to the court. Non-attendance necessitated an essoin [*essonium/ essonia*] that is, an excuse, either delivered in writing or more usually by a proxy [*plegius/ plegium*]. Only three consecutive essoins were permitted, their number being noted beside the person's name or in the margin, thus, first/1st, second/2nd, third/3rd [*primo/j°, secundo/ij° tercio/iij°*]. When a suitor defaulted in attendance [*fecit defaltam*] he was placed, like all offenders, at the mercy of the lord [*in misericordia domini*], and normally incurred an amercement (fine) for his non-appearance [*pro defalta/ pro defectu apparentie*]. The court might order [*preceptum est*] that the offender's goods be distrained [*distringatur*] or attached [*attachiatus*], the two terms being more or less synonymous, to ensure his future attendance or compliance with the court's decision. Persons placed in mercy had to find a pledge to guarantee the payment of the fine imposed. The amount of the amercement fixed by the assessors [*afferatores*] was often inserted over the offender's name in the court roll. The amount of the amercement was sometimes also written in the left-hand margin of the roll for ease of addition, with the words 'paid to the bailiff' [*solutos ballivio*] sometimes added. The grand total [*summa totalis*] of all fines and profits of the court was written at the end of the record of that particular court.

Manor court rolls note changes in tenancy such as a surrender [*sursum redditio*], escheat [*eschaeta*], and record the return of a tenement into the hand of the lord [*in manu domini*]; an incoming freehold tenant paid a relief [*relevium*] for his right to take over the tenement; an incoming servile tenant paid an entry fine [*fecit finem pro ingressu*] and swore fealty [*fidelitatem*] to the lord. Transfers of land are often noted as being accomplished by a symbolic act, the handing over of the land 'by rod' [*per virgam*] according to manorial custom [*secundum consuetudinem manerii*], and done in open court [*in plena curia*]. An heir succeeding to a tenement paid a heriot [*herrietum*], a tenant who demised, in other words leased [*dimisit*] a tenement to another person paid a fine [*gersumavit*] for the lord's approval [*pro licencia habenda*].

When the lord's financial interests had been dealt with, the manor court considered offences committed by the inhabitants of the manor. The reeve [*prepositus*], or the head tithingman [*decennarius/ franciplegius*] of each vill within the manor presented [*presentavit*] offenders. Offences included trespass with beasts [*transgressio cum averiis*], failure to scour ditches [*non obscuravit fossata sua*], failure to erect fences [*sepes*] or repair gaps [*rupture*].

Some lords had power to try serious offences, but most manor courts dealt only with minor matters. A manorial inhabitant who caused a brawl [*fecit affraiam*], or who assaulted [*verberavit*] another, was placed in mercy; his fine [*amerciamentum*] was heavier if he had drawn blood [*traxit sanguinem*].

Head tithingmen and even vills themselves could be fined for failure to enrol all adult males in a tithing [*decennaria*], and the person concerned was also amerced. Presentments of offenders were sometimes made by a jury of presentation [*presentatio*] or by chief pledges [*capitales plegii*]. In the roll of the view of frankpledge there was sometimes a special jury of twelve [*duodecimi*] 'for the king' [*pro rege*]. They delivered judgement [*veredictum*] following an inquiry [*inquisitio*] based on their knowledge of circumstances and the custom of the manor.

Among the most frequently found entries in manor court rolls are the names of persons, usually women, who had broken the laws regarding the price and quality of bread and ale [*fregerunt assisam panis/servisie*]. It is generally agreed, however, that this was in practice merely a form of licensing. Presentments of persons who had sold food [*victualia*] at an excessive price [*ad pretium excessivum*] or of bad quality are also found. Disputes between individuals often concerned pleas of land, debt, trespass, slander, dowries, etc. [*de placito terre/debiti/transgressionis/defamationis/dotis*]. The plaintiff [*querens/conquerens*] appeared in court [*optulit se*] against [*versus*] the defendant [*defendentem*], placed himself [*posuit se*] at the mercy of the lord and wagered his law [*vadiavit ad legem*], that is, brought compurgators to vouch for the truth of his accusations. Sometimes litigants were required to go to law six-handed [*sexto manu*], and to bring five compurgators to swear to the truth of his complaint, as well as himself. The plaintiff also brought pledges for prosecuting his case [*ad prosequendum/de prosequendo*] and the defendant likewise for replying to the charge [*ad respondendum*]. Such cases were a source of income to the lord, litigants paying to have judgement from the court [*ut habeat veredictum*] or for the lord's approval to settle out of court [*pro licencia concordanda*]. The person adjudged at fault paid the fine, sometimes in kind, for example six hens [*vj pullas*], and went away quit [*quietus*]. Often the case was deferred to the next court [*in respectu usque curiam proximam*].

Headings and Dates

The heading of a manor court roll usually gives the type of court [*Curia Baronis/Parva/Magna*, etc.], the day of the week [*die Lune, Martis*, etc.], with the word *die* in the ablative case and the name of the day in the genitive, on which the court was held [*tenta*] and the date expressed with reference to a saint's day [e.g. *in festo sancti Barnabe, post/ante festum sancte Lucie virginis*], followed by the regnal year as an ordinal [*in anno regni regis Edwardi tertii xij°*]. On the court rolls of a manor held by a monastery the name and year of office of the abbot is usually given [*anno abbatis Johannis vicesimo*]. Court rolls of the 16th century and later sometimes state the name of the lord of the manor, with his rank [*domini Oswaldi Mosley, baronetti*] and the name and rank of the steward of the manor in whose presence the court is held [*coram Johanne Lightwood, generoso*].

'Court of Keele held on Wednesday next before the feast of Saint Peter in Chains in the 29th year of the reign of King Edward III'.

Dates may be easily rendered into a modern form by using tables found in C. R. Cheney, *Handbook of Dates* (Royal Historical Society, 1945, reprinted with corrections 1970). Adopt the following procedure:
1. Ascertain what the regnal year is as an anno domini year, using the chapter on 'Rulers of England and Regnal Years'. Thus, for the example above, the 29th year of Edward III's reign ran from 25 January 1355 to 24 January 1356.

2. Referring to the chapter on 'Saints' Days and Festivals used in Dating' ascertain the date of the saint's day. Thus the feast of St Peter in Chains falls on 1 August. We are therefore in the year 1355.

3. Ascertain on which day of the week the saint's day fell. To do so turn to the 'Chronological Table of Easter Days' in Cheney; in 1355 Easter Day fell on 5 April. Now turn to the chapter 'Calendars for all possible dates for Easter' and find the table in which Easter Day falls on 5 April, in this case Table 15.

4. Find the day of the week on which the saint's day, 1 August, fell. This is a Saturday. The court was held on the Wednesday before this, i.e. 29 July 1355.

(Do not forget to consult the alternative columns for leap years.)

Exercise 1: Modernise the following dates.

(a)   Court held on Tuesday in the feast of St Cuthbert in the 21st year of the reign of Edward III.

(b)   Court held there on Wednesday after the feast of St Michael the Archangel in the 10th year of the reign of Henry VIII.

(c)   Court held on the morrow of the feast of St Mary Magdalen in the fourth year of the reign of Edward III.

(d)   Court held on Saturday in the feast of St Luke the Evangelist in the 17th year of the reign of king Richard II.

Exercise 2: Translate, modernising the date.

(a)   *Curia tenta apud ABC die Jovis proxima post festum sancti Barnabe apostoli anno domini mcclxxiij*

tenta: medieval Latin uses the past participle passive loosely; translate as 'held'. Note the final minim of a Roman numeral is always '*j*', as is the second of two '*i*'s at the end of a word, for example *manerij*.

(b)   *Curia parva tenta ibidem tertio die Novembris anno regni Henrici octavi dei gratia Anglie Francie et Hibernie regis fidei defensoris et in terra ecclesie Anglicane et Hibernice supremi capitis xxvij*

Only the contents of the particular court rolls themselves reveal the differences between *curia parva* and *curia magna*; note the string of genitive case-endings in apposition, and that it is 'English church' not 'Church of England'; the title 'Supreme Head' will of course only be found after Henry VIII's assumption of this title. Elizabeth continued to use this title, but in manor court rolls it fades out in the 17th century.

(c)   *Visus franciplegii cum curia tentus die Jovis proxima post festum Inventionis sancte crucis anno regni Henrici octavi xxxviij*

Here the past participle passive *tentus* has been extended from the original abbreviated word to agree with the masculine noun *Visus*, although an extension to a plural in the neuter is possible.

(d) *Curia baronis Willelmi Pargiter generosi firmarii prebende predicte tenta apud ABC*

Not infrequently, part of the endowment of a cathedral prebend was derived from the profits of a manor; in this case the manor has been farmed out to a lay holder.

(e) *Curia parva Humfridi Tyndall clerici sacre theologie doctoris tenta coram Johanne Martin generoso senescallo ibidem*

(f) *Curia et Leta tente ibidem die Lune proxima post festum Sancte Lucie Virginis anno regni regis Edwardi xiiij°*

This extract is taken from a court roll of the reign of Edward III.

Essoins and Pledges

The list of names of those making their essoins and of the persons who are standing proxy for the absent suitors usually follows immediately after the heading in a manor court roll.

Exercise 3: Translate.

(a) *Henricus le Sothne essoniat se per Robertum filium Hodi de communi secta j°*

Sothne should be translated as 'southerner'; later repetition of names will generally overcome any difficulties. Note the accusative case after *per* and the agreement of the adjective *communi* with ablative *secta*.

(b) *Robertus pistor essoniavit se per Ricardum clericum de secta curie primo*

Translate as 'the baker' and 'the clerk'.

(c) *Willelmus Adam essoniavit se per Hugonem messorem de eodem ij°*

de eodem, 'of the same' [suit of court].

(d) *Willelmus Fox essoniavit se per Willelmum Owen versus Margeriam sororem suam de placito terre primo. Plegii dicte Margerie querelam suam prosequendam sunt Robertus filius Radulphi et Nicholaus filius Radulphi*

In the family dispute brought before the court one of the parties has sent his excuses for not attending. The names of the defendant's pledges (sureties for any payments levied by the court) are given.

The frequently found expression, *querelam suam prosequendam*, uses 'for proceeding with her suit' the gerundive in preference to a gerund plus accusative.

(e) *Willelmus Docerill de apparentia per Willelmum Croket j°*

He sends his essoin for his non-appearance.

Suits

The order of business may vary from one court to another, but very often the consideration of suits, disputes between manorial inhabitants, follows the list of essoins. A few examples of suits are provided in the following exercises.

Exercise 4: Translate.

(a) *Johannes Kemster queritur de Agnete de Ragleye de placito quod occupavit domum et curtilagium contra voluntatem ad dampnum xl denariorum. Unde inquisitio <erat> et juratores dicunt quod non culpabilis. Ideo ipse in misericordia <est>*

Note the deponent verb *queritur*; it is often not possible to decide whether the extension of the abbreviation should be a noun, *querens*, or a verb, *queritur*. In this extract a jury of inquiry did not uphold the plaintiff's case and he was placed in mercy.

(b) *Adam Hichen queritur de Henrico Bust franciplegio de placito quod iniuste presentavit super ipsum quod ipse emendaret j fossatum ubi alii tenentes ville debent reparare*

An example of a suitor to the court complaining of an official wrongly charging him. Note the use of an imperfect subjunctive verb, *emendaret*. Frankpledge means the tithing-man as well as the group.

(c) *Abbas per attornatum suum querens versus Robertum le Hallsweyn de placito transgressionis qui non venit ideo districtus*

Here the abbot of a monastery who is also local lord of the manor brings a case of trespass to his own court. The defendant having failed to come in answer to the charge, the court orders that he be destrained, *districtus*, to appear – 'at the next court' being understood. Pleas of trespass are amongst the most frequently found cases in manor court rolls.

(d) *Ricardus Rond opponit se versus Henricum de Wylinton et Aliciam uxorem suam qui non veniunt et plegius fecit defaltam ideo melius districtus*

In this case not only the defendants but their pledge failed to turn up; *opponit se* is literally 'offered himself', appeared in court, ready with his witnesses and/or compurgators.

(e) *Willelmus Charle querens versus Robertum le laster de placito debiti plegii de prosequendo Johannes Hobbeson et Adam frater eius*

Pleas of debt are also commonly found in court rolls. Note the ablative gerund *prosequendo*.

(f) *Nicholaus le comber petit legem suam versus Johannem de Stapenhill de placito transgressionis unde consideratum est quod dictus Nicholaus habeat diem*

It was decided that he should 'have a day', meaning his case should be heard later, probably at the next court.

Presentments

Exercise 5: Translate.

(a) *Franciplegii de Bronston presentant quod Alana uxor Roberti Cuge vendidit servisiam contra assisam ideo in misericordia*

est, 'he is' or 'she is', is usually omitted after *misericordia.*

(b) *Idem presentant quod Henricus le cartwrighte braciavit contra assisam ideo in misericordia*

(c) *Franciplegii de Hornynglowe presentant quod Willelmus filius Radulphi Ernald qui debet sectam non venit*

(d) *Franciplegii de Burton presentant quod nichil sciunt*

'they know nothing', they have nothing to present. Note *nichil,* a commonly found variant of *nihil.*

(e) *xij juratores presentant quod Hugo (vjd.) de Menill et Robertus (vjd.) filius eius extraxerunt iniuste sanguinem de Roberto de Gresley qui attachiati fuerunt et invenerunt Johannem de Bursincot et Johannem de Stapenhill plegios ideo* etc.

A brawl between two prominent Midlands families in the earlier 14th century has involved bloodshed. The amount of the amercement or fine is written above the names and is here placed in brackets.

(f) *Item levatum fuit hutesium super eosdem iuste ideo in misericordia per plegios eosdem*

The hue and cry has been raised against the Meynells, of the previous entry. There was usually an inquiry after such an action, when a jury would decide whether the hue had been raised justly or unjustly.

(g) *Item inquisitio inter familiam Henrici de Fold et Aliciam uxorem Willelmi Orme ponitur in respectu usque sabbato proximo videlicet de hutesio levato*

(h) *Galfridus de Monte calumpniatur quia destruit herbagium vicinorum cum averiis extraneorum*

Copyhold Transactions in Manorial Court Records

Copyhold was a tenure originally based upon custom and upon the will of the lord of the manor. In the earlier middle ages the tenant occupied land within the manor in return for rendering various labour services to the lord of that manor. These tasks included the requirement to work for so many days a week on the lord's demesne land, and perform tasks appropriate to the local agrarian economy and the season, such as ploughing, harrowing, sowing, harvesting and carrying. The volume and variety of such tasks was fixed by local manorial custom, and although it was not impossible for the lord to alter these conditions custom had, in effect, almost the force of law. From as early as the 12th century there is evidence that some lords found it to their advantage to commute labour services into a money rent and this process was speeded up by the labour shortages caused by the Black Death of 1349. By the end of the 14th century labour services had mostly disappeared, and had been replaced by what was known as copyhold tenure. Such land was similar to freehold in that it could be bought, sold and mortgaged, but the title to the holding was an entry in the manor court rolls, of which the tenant had a copy, hence the term 'copyhold'. Any transaction concerning copyhold land had to go through the manor court and be recorded on the court rolls. By the early or mid-17th century, with the decay of other functions of the manor, copyhold transactions are often the only matters found recorded in the rolls. Until 1733 the rolls legally had to be written in Latin but the use of English is often found before that date. In the next century the steady decline in the number of copyholders reduced the volume of business concerning this tenure in the manor courts. It was not until 1922, however, that copyhold tenure was statutorily abolished, and for purposes of local historical and genealogical research many court rolls of the later centuries often provide much information. The Latin, handwriting and the abbreviations encountered are likely to present fewer obstacles to understanding than the often lengthy and repetitive legal terminology in which the manor court copyhold transactions are recorded.

Local variations in procedure are common but typically the copyhold transaction as recorded in a manor court roll is as follows. After the title of the court [*Curia parva/baronis,* etc.] comes the name of the lord, his Christian name and rank in the genitive case [*Henrici Hollis Armigeri*]; this is followed by the date expressed as a day and month in a regnal year [*anno domini nostri Caroli dei gratia Anglie etc. xxj°*]. Note that the ordinal is not next to the word *anno* but is placed after the abbreviated royal title; the steward of the lord of the manor, before whom [*coram*] the court is held, is cited in the ablative case [*Willelmo Babington, senescallo*].

The names of persons essoining themselves, if any, are then listed; these often include gentlemen and others living outside the manor but who have copyhold lands within the manor. The fines for non-attendance were an extra source of income to the lord of the manor.

The names of 12 or sometimes more men to act as the homage [*homagium*] – the body of tenants acting as a jury at the court, are then listed and shown as 'sworn' [*jurati*].

Then follows the record of the particular transaction involving copyhold land, usually a sale or an heir seeking to succeed to the holding. The occupant, A. B., came into the court [*ad hanc curiam venit A. B.*] in his own person [*in propria persona sua*], claimed that he held the title [*pretendit habere titulum*] and with the lord's permission [*per licenciam domini*] surrendered [*remisit/relaxavit/quietumclamavit*] all his title to the holding to another named person. The surrender was often couched in words which attempted to close all possible legal loopholes, including all present, past or possible future rights of the previous holder [*totum jus et clameum que habet habuit vel in futuro habere potuerit*]. This was often reinforced by a warranty clause in which the holder renounced for himself and his heirs [*ipse et heredes sui*] any possibility of a future legal claim to the title [*de cetero exigere vel vendicare*]. Legally the copyhold was surrendered into the hands of the lord [*in manus domini*]. The person to whom it was surrendered also appeared at the same court [*in ista eadem curia venit*] and received it from the lord [*cepit de domino manerii predicti*], who, through his steward [*per senescallum suum*], granted him seisin i.e. possession [*ei concessit seisinam*]. In some manors the rolls record the symbolic handing over of a stick [*per virgam*] to mark the change of occupant. The incoming copyholder paid a fine to the lord [*fecit finem*] at his entry [*ad ingressum*], did fealty [*fecit fidelitatem*] and was admitted tenant [*et admissus inde tenens*]. The fine payable by a new tenant who was not an heir was called a relief [*relevium*]. Its level was normally fixed by local custom [*secundum consuetudinem manerii*]. It could be determined arbitrarily by the lord though the common law courts had held that the fine must be reasonable. Copyhold is discussed at length in W. Holdsworth, *A History of English Law* (Methuen, 2nd edition, reprinted 1966), vol. vii, pages 296-312, and title deeds generally in N. W. Alcock, *Old Title Deeds* (Phillimore, 1986).

It was the duty of the homage to report on oath [*super sacramentum suum*] when a customary tenant [*customarius tenens*] had died since the last court [*obijt citra ultimam curiam*] having been in possession of a tenement [*seisitus de uno tenemento*]. They then stated who was the heir of the deceased [*defuncti*] and whether a heriot [*heriettum*] or its customary financial equivalent fell due to the lord.

To these essential features of copyhold transactions found in manor court rolls is often added extra detail which is useful for the historical reconstruction of the local scene. The repetition of phrases necessary for legal purposes often makes translation a lengthy process, but the Latin is usually not heavily abbreviated in the later manor court rolls. The following transcribed extracts for translation provide examples of most of the technical vocabulary likely to be encountered.

Exercise 6: Translate.

(a) *Ad hanc curiam venerunt Edwardus Breerton de Morrey infra manerium de ABCD predicto et Anna Breerton uxor eius in propriis personis suis et coram Zacharia Babington generoso senescallo predicto pretendunt habere titulum in quodam prato vocato Dan Meadowe*

Note the string of ablatives after *coram*. Nothing new in vocabulary here.

(b) *Et super hoc in ista eadem curia venerunt prefati Jacobus Wright et Elizabetha Wright in propriis personis suis et ceperunt de domino manerii premissa predicta quibus dominus per senescallum suum predictum concessit eis inde seisinam per virgam secundum consuetudinem manerii predicti*

Do not expect any punctuation in the manuscripts; *eis* is logically unnecessary after *quibus*.

(c) *...ipsi Edwardus, Anna et Elizabetha nec heredes suorum nec aliquid eorum nec aliquis aliud nomine eorum vel aliquid eorum aliquod ius titulum interesse vel clameum in prato predicto de cetero exigere vel vendicare potuerunt sed ab omni accione juris seu clameum fuerunt exclusi*

The legal phrases are piling up; scribes are not always consistent in their use of verbs in such complex strings of clauses and it is sometimes clearer to break up the paragraph into shorter sentences when you translate.

(d) *...Habendum et tendendum premissa predicta prefato Johanni Illsley heredibus et assignatis suis ad voluntatem domini secundum consuetudinem manerii predicti per redditus, reparaciones et omnia alia servicia inde prius debita et de iure consueta et ad decessum predicti Johannis Illsley optimum animalium sive bovum pro herrietto vel iij li. ad eleccionem domini manerii predicti. Et dat domino pro fine ad ingressum 15 li. et fecit fidelitatem et admissus est inde tenens in forma predicta*

Here the entry includes the '*Habendum*' clause found in title deeds. John Illsley, the heir, not only pays a heriot, whether in kind or money at the lord's choice, but also pays a heavy fine.

Transcription of Printed Extracts with Abbreviations

Abbreviations and their extension

Abbreviations were much used in manorial court rolls for the sake of speed, to save space and sometimes out of sheer habit. The terms used were so familiar and their abbreviations so standard that the meaning was seldom in doubt. The scrupulous care shown by scribes writing important legal documents is not, however, to be expected from those who compiled the court rolls, especially if these exist in the form of court papers executed hastily on the spot, or drafted beforehand in outline and added to and amended as the court proceeded. In some cases both the court papers and the engrossed court rolls exist, the latter more carefully written but the former often with more information.

Once the beginner has mastered the standard forms taken by abbreviation and contraction marks, then transcription is a matter of acquaintance with the technical terms and vocabulary of the manor court roll. Some degree of skill in transcribing documents written in English is desirable before the transcription of Latin court rolls is attempted, and beginners may wish to practise on manorial records of the Commonwealth period and after 1734, when court rolls were written in English, before they tackle Latin. These notes are not a substitute for the works on palaeography listed earlier but are intended to help beginners to acquire confidence to attempt their own local records; experience and practice are by far the best way to learn, even if many gaps are left at first in the transcription. Students should attempt to read whole phrases as soon as possible rather than struggle with individual letters. If a blockage occurs then the next word or words will often provide the clue to the transcription. Look to see what follows, guess what the word/s 'ought' or are likely to be, and then check carefully.

Scribes normally indicated when they had omitted letters or contracted a word by special marks, strokes or signs. A word is said to be suspended when a letter or letters at the end of the word is/are missing, and words in which letters in the middle are omitted are said to be contracted. The most frequently found abbreviation marks are as follows:

'	An apostrophe, thus: *q'd; quod.*
$\bar{u}, \tilde{w}$	A straight or curled line over the middle or end of the word, thus: *cū* or *cw̃*; *cum.*
p , *ꝑ*	A line through the tail or descender of a '*p*', which takes two forms, thus: *p per* or *par* and *ꝑ pro.*
ꝰ , ˋ	A mark like a large comma following a '*p*' thus: *pꝰ* indicating the omission of '*re*', e.g. *pꝰmissa; premissa.* A sign rather like an Arabic figure *9*, often above the normal level of writing, indicating omission of *-us* e.g. *ipiˢ; ipsius.*
ꝯ	A similar sign at the beginning of a word indicating *con-* e.g. *ꝯsueta.*
ᵗ	A 'superior' or superscript letter placed above the normal level of writing indicates the omission of other letters, e.g. *qᵗre; quare.*
ꝝ	The 'Arabic-2 small r', rather like a florid figure four, thus: *ꝝ* used to indicate the letters *-rum* of the genitive plural of the noun, for instance *eoꝝ; eorum.*

e A mark at the end of an abbreviated word rather like an *'e'* with a long tail, thus:
e indicating omission of *-es* or *-is* e.g. *omne* ; *omnes.*

z A mark like a printed superior *'z'* meaning *'-ur'* often indicating the ending of
the 3rd person singular and other forms of the verb in the passive voice e.g.
*vocat*ᶻ, vocatur.

3 A mark like a cursive *'z'*, thus: *3* indicating the omission of *-us* or *-et*, for
instance *quib3* ; *quibus, deb3* ; *debet*; after *'q'* it also means *-ue.*

These brief notes will serve to get you started. A slightly fuller treatment is contained in the
appendix, and the works on palaeography listed above should be consulted as necessary.

Exercise 7: Transcribe the following with the aid of the translations which follow, showing
your extensions in brackets.

(a) *Q'd Ph' pistor deb3 ixs.vjd. Ric' Meysey It' deb3 iiijs.vjd. Matheo de Lodelowe It' d3 dño ijs.vjd.
q⁴r' adjudicat' est ad carcerē quousqȝ solvit totū vel inven'it pleg'*

That Philip the baker owes 9s. 6d. to Richard Meysey. Likewise he owes 3s. 6d. to Matthew de
Ludlow. Likewise he owes to the lord 2s. 6d. wherefore he is condemned to prison until he
pays the whole or shall have found pledges.

(Remember to use the dative of person to whom the debt is owed and the future perfect for
the last verb.)

(b) *Edit' q' fuit ux' Henr' recupat de debito suo viijs.jd. de Johē Karles ad solvend' in festo b'i
Michaele*

Edith who was the wife of Henry recovers of her debt 8s. 1d., of John Karles to be paid at the
feast of the blessed Michael [Michaelmas].

(Don't miss the line through the tail of the *'p'*, the accusative gerund, and the final
abbreviation.)

(c) *Mᵈ q'd Johēs de Stretton clĩcus ve' i' plena cur' et fec' fidelitatē p q'dā acr' t're arabtĩs q'd habu' de
Ric' de Stretton*

Let it be noted that John of Stretton, clerk, came into full [open] court and did fealty for a
certain acre of arable land which he had from Richard of Stretton.

(Note the superscript letter *'d'* of the first word indicating omission of letters and the
modification of *'p'* in line two. Otherwise the scribe uses mostly apostrophe commas.)

Here now are some examples of abbreviated words commonly found in the headings of
manorial court rolls. Abbreviation signs found in the original are indicated in the
transcriptions which follow chiefly by apostrophe commas and straight lines.

Cur'; Cur<ia>, court. This is an example of suspension, where the scribe has indicated the
omission of the last two letters by a general abbreviation sign.
p'va; p<ar>va, small. An example of contraction.
ibm̄; ib<ide>m, in the same place. The commonest sign of suspension or contraction is a
horizontal line above the small letters of the word. This often passes through the ascenders
of *'b'*, *'l'* etc.

defensor'; *defensor<is>*, defender [of the faith]. Part of the royal title after 1521 when the pope awarded it to Henry VIII for his pamphlet *Assertio Septem Sacramentorum.*
r'r'; *r<egni>*; *r<egis>*, in the reign of king ... An extreme form of suspension, with only the initial letters given.

Exercise 8: Transcribe, extending the abbreviations and showing these extensions within brackets; then translate, modernising the dates.

   Do not look at the answers until you have attempted each extract, no matter how many blank spaces you may have left. Account to yourself for the grammar and agreements, which you may find tedious at first but worthwhile in the long run.

(a)   *Vis' franc' cu͡ cur' tent' ib͞m die Jovis px' post fest' Inventōīs s'c'e cruc' anno regni reg' Henr' octavi xxj°*

Note how the *'u'* of *cu* curls back to make the abbreviation mark. The loop of the *'p'* curls back before it crosses the tail to indicate *p<ro>*, here part of *p<ro>x<ima>*.

(b)   *Cur' man'ij p'd'ti tent' ib͞m die Sab'i px' ante fest' s'c'i mathei in estate anno r'r' Henrici sept'i post conq'm Anglie sextodecimo*

The term *post conquestum* is found regularly up to the end of the 16th century, after which its use diminishes.

(c)   *Cur' Baron' Philippi Pargiter Ar' ib͞m tent' p man'io p'd' anno regni d'ni n'ri Caroli scdi' nunc Regis Anglie etc. xxxvj° cor' D. Beech Sen'*

From a later 17th-century court roll. A few new words and abbreviations here: don't forget to extend *Ar'* into the genitive case and *Sen'* into the ablative. The marks of abbreviation in the original are not very full.

Once the abbreviations of the technical vocabulary of essoins and pledges are familiar, probably only personal names will cause difficulty. Read the previous section on essoins again, and then attempt the following exercises.

Exercise 9: Transcribe, extend the abbreviations showing your extensions in brackets, and translate.

(a)   *Rob' pistor es͞s se p Ric'm clic͞u de secta cur' p'mo*

From a mid-13th-century roll in which the scribe tends to use a straight line to indicate the abbreviations. Note the bar through the tail of the *'p'*, this time, which extends it to *per* because it is not a continuation of the descender itself, coming from below, thus: *ꝑ*. Again it is to be transcribed *per.* The parish priest, *clericus*, often acted as a proxy for absent suitors.

(b)   *Margareta Hynckley deb' sect' huius cur' et fecit se essoniari*

An example of one of the many variations found in the way essoins are recorded; note the passive infinitive, but you need not show this in the translation.

(c) *Esson' Henr' se de c̄o̅i̅ p̄ Mauriciu̅ filiu̅ suu̅ Rad̄s̄ Wyllok se de eod' p̄ Ad' Skipp*

Sometimes essoins are listed with a general heading in the left-hand margin. Refer back to the fully transcribed essoins if you have difficulty.

(d) *Witt̄s̄ Fox esson' se p̄ Witt̄m̄ Owen v's Margeriam soror' de p̄'to terre j°*

Brother versus sister in a family squabble over land which has been brought to the manor court. The plaintiff has sent an essoin. Note the abbreviation mark through the two *'l's* of *Willelmus* and *Willelmum*.

Extending the abbreviations of presentments is largely a matter of experience. The following exercise provides a variety of examples.

Exercise 10: Transcribe, extend the abbreviations showing your extensions in brackets, and translate.

(a) *Thomas Halley dec' ib̄m̄ present' Antoniu̅ Grey ijd. et Rob'tu̅ Grey p̄ def'tu apparant'. I'o quilib't eoʏ̣ in mi̅a̅ d̄n̄i̅. Et eleg' in officio dec' Joh̄e̅m̄ Sale jur'*

Note the abbreviations of *ideo* and *eorum*. The subject of the verb *eleg'* is presumably 'They', i.e. the court as a whole, and John Sale is the accusative object. A passive voice construction, which in this case would have been *Johannes Sale electus est*, is often found in the election of manorial officials.

(b) *It'm p̄'sent' q'd Ric̄u̅s̄ Porter (ijd.) fec' affraiam sup̄ Johannem Cartwright contra pacem etc. I'o ip̄'e in m̄i̅a̅.*

Lengthy legal phrases are often omitted, using instead *'etc'*. Note the omission of the *'s'* in *ipse*.

(c) *Vered'c'm xij (mi) Qui quidem jur' de div'sis artic'lis cur' tangent' on'ati ven' et affirmant om'ia et sing'la p̄ officiarios p̄'d'c'os supius p̄'sent' fore vera et dic' q'd officiarii p̄'d'c'i bene et fidelit' p̄'sentav'unt et null' fec'unt concelament' ad notitiam jur' p̄'d'*

Very heavily abbreviated. The jury of 12 men (note the genitive ordinal) were 'charged' with the articles touching the court. Extend *tangent'* as a present participle agreeing with *artic'lis*, and *cur'* as its accusative object. The use of *fore*, the future infinitive, is unusual. Extend *null'* to agree with *concelament'*.

(d) *Et ult'ius p̄'sent' q'd Edwardus Aston miles qui de d'no tenuit p̄ copiam rot'li s'c'd'm cons' man'ij p̄'d'c'i un' messuagiu̅ ac prata eidem mes' spectant' in Magna Heywood diem clausit extre'um citra ultim' cur' post cui'mort' accid' d'no un' tauru̅ p̄'tij xxxiijs.ivd. no'i̅'e h'ietti*

This extract from a 16th-century court roll contains a number of standard phrases concerning land transfers. The jury are reporting that by the death of a tenant – 'he closed his last day' – a bull worth 33s. 4d. falls due to the lord in the name of heriot. Ensure you extend *spectant'* correctly to agree with the noun it qualifies. The construction with *accid<it> d<omi>no* may be found with the heriot expressed in the nominative case, 'a bull falls due to the lord', or with *accidit* used as a transitive verb followed by the heriot in the accusative case, *un<um> tauru<m>* – as in Example 4(d) below. Follow the scribe's precedent, if any.

Extending the abbreviations found in copyhold entries in manuscript court rolls should not cause undue difficulty, once the student is familiar with the general vocabulary of such transactions. They are the same as found in manor court rolls generally and there are fewer of them usually. The following examples cover most of the new and technical words in such documents.

Exercise 11: Transcribe, extending the abbreviations within brackets, then translate.

(a) *Ad hanc Cur' ven' Johes Welles ar. þ Radẃ Right Attornat' eius et sursẃ reddit in manus dñi man'ij p'd̄ unẃ cottagiẃ et unẃ clausẃ anglice a Croft ībm ptineñ nuþ in tenura Robti Turner defunct'*

The subject is John Welles so that *ven'* can only extend into a singular form. This applies also to *sursẃ reddit*. Note the abbreviated form of *armiger*. Welles, an important local gentleman, has sent his attorney to represent him. The extension of *ptineñ* could be to a neuter singular or plural.

(b) *... unẃ messuagiẃ sive tenementẃ cẃ ptiñtñ iaceñ et existeñ in Morrey End infra man'iẃ p'd' ad opus et usẃ Witti Crooke et Cat'ine Crooke ux' eius þ et durant' termino vite naturalis eoɤ et eoɤ diutius viventiẃ*

Many of the abbreviations here are in the form of suspensions of the final letter/s. The terminal *'m'* is shown as a backward curling stroke, often hooked. There is an example of the superior straight line abbreviation mark in *Witti*, the modification of the letter *'þ'* and the mark signifying the genitive plural ending *-rum*.

(c) *... unẃ cottagiẃ cẃ ptineñ scituat' et existeñ in ABCD p'd' cẃ oib₃ domib₃ edificijs horreis stabul' gardin' pomar' cẃ puteis corarijs anglice Tanffats ...*

Note the succession of plural ablative nouns and the abbreviation mark for *-us*. Sometimes the scribe writes the whole word in full. Thoughtfully he provided his own translation of *puteis corarijs*.

(d) *... ac uñā pastur' sive croftẃ eid' ptinen' et adiacen' ac unam pec̄i sive pcella' vasti adiacen' eid' cottagio*

(e) *... ac unẃ furnaciu' vel humitoriẃ (anglice one kiln house or Tanyard) ut nunc abuttat anglice as it is now bounded et uñā mandra' stant' suþ sex postibus anglice a hovel standing upon six posts...*

Later court rolls frequently give the English for some special word or phrase.

a)

b)

c)

d)

e)

Example 1

Transcription and Translation of Short Manuscript Extracts

The previous exercises have provided a first and general acquaintance with the vocabulary and constructions to be found in manorial court rolls and the main sorts of abbreviations to be expected. The next stage deals with short, fairly easy extracts from actual manuscripts. Transcribe Examples 1(a) to 1(e), extending the abbreviations within brackets, then translate, also modernising the date. Here are some notes to help you.

Example 1(a)
There is a line filler at the end of line one; a second terminal *'i'* is shown as a *'j'*; the bold superior curved mark following the *'p'* in the first word of line two almost invariably indicates the omission of *'re'*; the last word of line three is *annoq<ue>*; don't miss the series of ablatives after *coram*.

Example 1(b)
This is taken from an early 14th-century abbey manor court roll. Initial capital letters are often the most difficult to read, and an alphabet may be useful at this stage. Ablative case-endings of place names are usually shown in documents by an apostrophe comma, possibly because the full name and gender of the place-name was not known, and this practice should be followed in your transcriptions. Study the complex letter *'w'* of the hands of this period and the scribe's variant spelling of the Latin word for 'evangelist'. Take care to distinguish the ablative and genitive forms of the ordinal '3rd'.

Example 1(c)
The scribe seems to be using the abbreviated form of the adjective *proxima*, which suggests that he thinks of *dies* as feminine, although more often it is masculine.

Example 1(d)
Note the abbreviation p° , which differs from previous forms encountered. A 'Confessor' is a saint who did not suffer martyrdom. The year referred to was 1328.

Example 1(e)
This is from a manor court roll of 1259. The hand is clear but correct transcription needs experience, especially of the *'a'* and *'d'* as in *apud*. Note the form of the capital *'R'* in *Reg<ni>*and of the capital *'H'* in, *H<enrici>*, very characteristic of the period.

The next exercises combine headings with essoins. Re-read the earlier sections on vocabulary and form. Then transcribe, with extensions of abbreviated words in brackets, and translate, again modernising the dates. Do not spend too much time struggling with unusual surnames; they would become familiar with repetition. Try to transcribe them, check your answers, then repeat the exercise in a day or so.

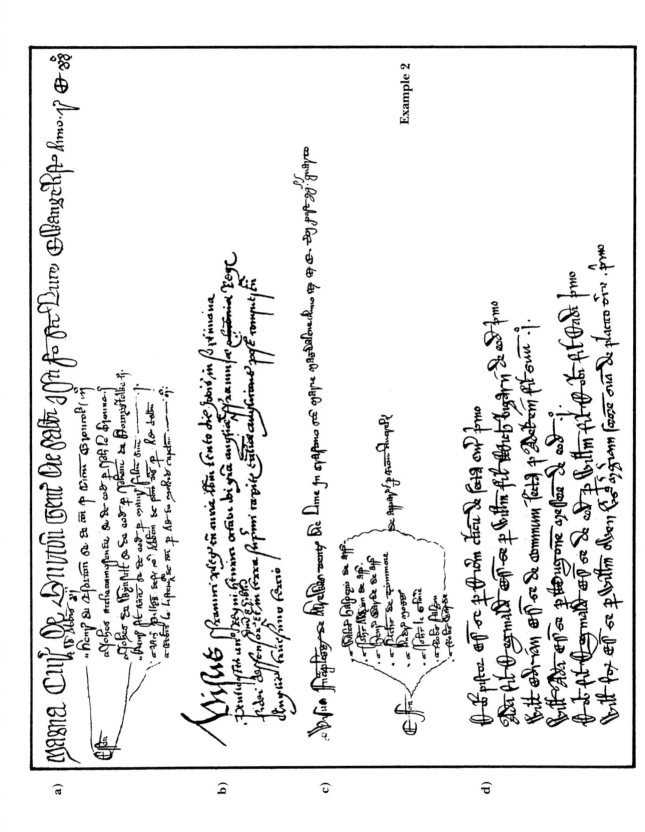

Example 2

Example 2(a)
The heading gives the year of office of the abbot as well as the regnal year.

Line 2   *at the tounesende.*

Line 3   *Wynsull,* with the complex 'W' twice more in this line. Study the forms of the
                letters in the last word *Hornyglowe,* writing them out for yourself.

Line 4   Upper case 'R' is a deceptive letter in this early 14th-century hand.

Line 5   *Pilly<n>g* with the omission indicated by an abbreviation mark; *def' v^s* is *deficit
                versus.*

Do not forget the Roman numeral at the end of most lines.

Example 2(b)
This is an extract from a view of frankpledge on an Essex manor in the reign of Henry VIII:
the scribe had endeavoured, perhaps wisely, to get the royal title correct. Occasionally he
uses the classical *'ae'* in the genitive case ending, but in line one one would grammatically
require *tentus* to agree with *visus* in the nominative case. It is not certain whether the scribe
has written *Fraunci* or *Frannci.*

Example 2(c)
Another extract from a view of frankpledge, this time from a manor in Staffordshire *tempore*
Edward III. All the essoins are brought by one man, Richard Averel. The writing is so small
that you would have to guess at some of the names until they could be confirmed from
previous or subsequent examples, but this cramped style is not infrequently encountered,
and accordingly is included.

Example 2(d)
No surprises here in the technical terms.
Line 3-4   Initial capital letters may prove difficult. For example, in line three the 'N' in
                Nich<olai> is somewhat similar to the 'H' of *Hugone<m>* in line four.
Line 7   The name is *Owen.*

This is probably the most difficult hand you have yet encountered. Do not be dismayed if you
did not do very well.

a)

b)

a)

b)

c)

d)

Examples 3 and 4

Example 3(a)
Manorial officials were often elected immediately after the jury were sworn in. This entry shows one of the functions of the reeve. Plenty of abbreviations to extend.

Example 3(b)
A similar entry, this time the election and swearing of abbey grangers at *Schob<nall>* and *Stretton*, and incidentally throwing more light on the abbey economy.

Presentments of offenders were made by manorial officials or by a manorial jury. Such entries usually provide much information useful in local history research. The words and phrases used are repeated so often that you will have little difficulty in transcription.

Example 4(a)
This comes from a mid-17th-century manor court roll, written in a rather flamboyant hand. Be careful of the lower case *'a'* with its ascending stroke, and note the combination of letters *'st'* in the third word. The last three words, in translation, are 'that all [is] well'.

Example 4(b)
In this entry, from a manor court roll of 1325, a number of persons are listed for having committed the same offence, i.e. trespassing with their geese (and in the last line, with calves) in the lord's cornfield and meadow. Read the section on vocabulary in the Introduction again to familiarise yourself with the form of words. You will find the names difficult to transcribe: try first before you look at the answers, then, after a day or so, try again.

Example 4(c)
From a 17th-century roll, and not easy to read. Fences between two fields must be maintained, under penalty.

Line 2   Note: *iuxta* 'according'.

Example 4(d)
A fairly modern hand, from the later 17th century, recording that one of the customary tenants of the manor has died and that a heriot therefore falls due to the lord of the manor.

Line 2   Be careful of the extension of *defunct*: with what does it agree?
Line 4   *bovum*, more often *bovem*, the accusative of *bos*; *bovis* (m.), 'ox', and here the scribe has treated *accidit* as a transitive verb requiring a direct object.

There now follows a series of examples of entries from manor court rolls recording copyhold transactions brought before the court, all in the same hand, to promote familiarity with this type of entry and confidence with the vocabulary. The rolls date from the mid-17th century. Once you are able to recognise the standard abbreviations such documents will present little difficulty in transcription; the main problems lie in the complex legal jargon and repetitiveness. If you have copyhold transactions in your own court rolls, work steadily through them, no matter how tedious the process may be.

a) Ad hanc Cur[iam] ven[it] Willi[elmu]s Normanfell de Nor[th]hampton in
Com[itatu] p[re]d[ic]to Mercer in p[ro]pria p[er]sona sua Et sursu[m] redd[idit] in manib[us] d[omi]ni
Mawdy p[re]d[ic]t[i] quatuor dorabr[atas] terra[m] earum in quadam Clausa vocat[a] [la]
Leys Dischguin nup[er] in tenura sive occupac[i]on[e] Thom[e] Ruyton
ad opus et usu[m] ip[s]i[us] Thom[e] Ruyton

b) Ad hanc Cur[iam] ven[it] Samuel Lathropp de leigh in Com[itatu] Stoff[ord] p[re]d[ic]t[o]
et cepit de d[omi]no Mawdy p[re]d[ic]t[o] p[re]dict[a]t[as] duas Messuagior[um] sive
Tentor[um] c[um] p[er]tin[entiis] vocat[a] Halway[en] things iacen[t] in Nor[th] End
infra Manu[m] de Yocall p[re]d[ic]t[a] ac medietat[em] vnius Cottagii ac
medietat[em] omni[um] domor[um] Edificior[um] gardin[orum] hor[re]or[um] pomar[um] croft[...]
terr[...] tentor[um] p[ra]t[a] pascua et pastur[...] c[um] p[er]tin[entiis] ac p[er]tin[entibus]
sive aliquo modo p[er]tin[ent] in Yocall p[re]d[ic]t[a]

c) Iacen[t] et tenent[ur] p[re]d[ic]t[a] medietat[em] duar[um]
Messuag[iorum] sive Tentor[um] p[re]d[ic]t[a] ac medietat[em] Cottag[ii] p[re]d[ic]t[i] ac
medietat[em] omni[um] et singlor[um] p[re]miffor[um] p[re]d[ic]t[orum] c[um] p[er]tin[entiis] p[re]fat[o]
S[amue]l Lathropp h[e]r[e]d[ibus] et affign[atis] fuis[...] vnaq p[er]tin[entiis]
ad voluntate[m] d[omi]ni fec[un]d[u]m ten[ore]m Mawdy p[re]d[ic]t[i] q[ui] Reddit ar[...] p[er] ann[um]
et cetera al[ia] fervic[i]a inde p[ri]us debit[a] et de iure consuet[a].
Et ad div[ers]o[rum] ip[s]i[us] Samuel duo ip[...] optimis fuis animalib[us]
sive bonis p[ro] heriott[...] q[ui] utroq Messuag[ium] sive Tent[orum] c[um]
p[er]tin[entiis] vel quinq[ue] librous ad ele[c]c[i]on[em] d[omi]ni Mawdy p[re]d[ic]t[i]
Et dedit d[omi]no de fine ad ingr[essum] Et admiff[u]s eft
inde Tenent[ur] ferit[...] d[omi]no fidelitate[m]

Example 5(a)

Line 1   Notice the abbreviation mark signifying *'er'* in *Wolv<er>hampton* – which looks like a modern *'u'* or *'n'* continued by an upward backward-curling stroke.

Line 2   *mercer*

Line 3   Read *iacen<tes>*, a difficult word because of the *'c'* and *'e'*, the latter looking like a *'t'*; this is a present participle in the accusative plural agreeing with 'four acres'; ensure your extension of *vocat'* agrees with the noun it refers to.

Line 4   *disp<er>sim; occupac<i>one*, the letter *'i'* being invariably omitted in words containing the combination of letters *'ion'*; note the very hastily formed terminal *'e'* of this word, a characteristic shape.

Example 5(b)

Line 1   The last word is *gen<erosus>*.

Line 2   Note the 'Arabic-2 small r', denoting the letters *'rum'* of the genitive plural.

Line 3   *halswayne things,* i.e. tenements attaching to the office of hall swain or servant, although the office had long since disappeared.

Line 5   There is no abbreviation mark for the genitive plural of 'gardens'.

Line 6   *spectan<tibus>* qualifying *p<er>tinen<tiis>*.

Example 5(c)

Line 7   You will often find *ipius* without any abbreviation mark to show the omission of *'s'*.

Line 11   *fecitq<ue>*

Ad hanc Cur venit Johes Plummer in ppia psona
Sua in plen Cur Sursum reddidit in manus Dni Manij
p dict p virgam secdm consuetud Manij pdict un Dolam
prati cu ptid in Burway Meadow jaceñ Supplongmoore
ibm. & un ab Dolam prati in codm prato jaceñ
Sup le Smooth ibm int Terr olim Willi Daniell ex una
pto et terr Dni Manij p d ex alt ple un ab Dolam
prati jaceñ in prato vocat Longlakefttterr ibm olim
Henci Smith ex una pte & terr Johis Mousley ex alt
pte et un ab Dat prati in eadem prato jaceñ int
terr olim p d Henci Smith ex una pte et terr hered
Thome Bayley Defunct ex alter pte cum pted ad opus
et ulium Johis Shemonds Hered & assignator Suoding etud
Et Sup hoc in ista eadm Curia ven p d Johes Shemonds
in ppia psona Sua & in plen Cur petit admitti huc
pmissis p d cu ptid cui Dnus Manij p d p Senium
Suum p dict concessit inde seiam p virgam sedm
consuetud Manij p d et tenend pmissa pte
cu ptid p fat Johi Shemonds Hered et assignat Suis
Imppetuu ad voluntat Dni sedm consuet Man p d p
reddit Herriot at ab servic inde prius debit p de jure
consuet. Et dat Dno. p fine ad Ingress
Et post hos pclamacones inde serius fact secdm consuet.
Manij p d Admiss est inde & fec Dno fidelitat &c

The Transcription and Translation of Harder Manuscript Extracts

Now follow examples of the kind of extracts you are likely to encounter in the process of research. If necessary leave blanks in your first transcription until repetition of a word or phrase brings enlightenment. If there are many blanks at first *nil desperandum:* most manor court rolls present some problems even to the experienced palaeographer. In order to maintain interest you need not initially do the whole of each extract, but do so eventually, because the documents have been selected to provide a comprehensive vocabulary. If you have manorial records of your own which you wish to transcribe and translate, make a start on them now, comparing the vocabulary and forms of abbreviation with those in this book: there is no substitute for your own experience, not even this book. Finally, a tip: when you think you know a word, look it up!

Example 6

This is a useful document to practise on because it is written in an almost modern hand but contains many technical words found in copyhold documents and plenty of abbreviations. (The latter are also treated in a special appendix at the end of the book.) Three old manor court procedures are found in this document, the symbolic act of transfer 'by the rod', proclamations on the admission of a tenant and the act of fealty.

Line 1	Note the bar through the tail of the first *'p'* and the omission of a contraction mark after the second.
Line 3	Ensure you get the correct extension of the noun after the preposition *s<e>c<un>d<u>m;* the last two words in the line form the accusative object of the verb 'surrenders' in line two.
Line 4	The last word is *jacen̄* a present participle agreeing with a preceding noun; think it through before turning to the answer.
Line 5	The scribe has scratched out one word and substituted another. When a transcription is in doubt because of some such alteration or because of fading or damage the editiorial convention is to leave three dots ...
Line 7	*p<ar>te;* note the way in which the location of a tenement is described as lying *int<er>* other named holdings.
Line 13	Ensure you extend all the genitive plurals here.
Line 15	Note the passive infinitive construction; don't fail to extend *tenen̄* as the nominative complement of a copulative verb. For accurate transcriptions you do need to be aware of the grammar.
Line 16	*p<er> s<enes>callum*
Line 17	The long walking stick *'s'* is followed by another *'s'; sei<sin>am,* i.e. 'seisin', the possession of a property, is the feminine accusative object of *concessit.*
Line 18	The word inserted between the lines is presumably *predicti,* but is almost illegible; *H<ab>end<um> et tenend<um> p<re>missa p<re>d<icta>.*
Line 19	Remember that the name of the new holder of the property and his heirs, etc., is in the dative case.
Line 21	*debita et*
Line 22	The amount of the entry fine is omitted in the original.

Examples 7 and 8

Example 7

A difficult hand. This extract is probably much more like the actual documents you will encounter than the carefully selected extracts so far provided. The abbreviations and vocabulary, however, are standard. In this document the tithing men [*decennarii*] are making their presentments to the court of absentees, persons selling food at excessive prices, ale brewers who have broken the assize, etc.

Line 1   Learn to recognise this initial capital '*N*' in the first name; capital '*T*' of *Thomam* is also a difficult letter.

Note how the fines are inserted over the names of offenders.

Line 2-3   *tenet co<mmun>e<m> hospitiu<m>; victual<ia>*

Line 4   Widow Assheton is one of the common brewers of ale: Can you get the Latin now?

Line 6   The first word is *carnis*.

Example 8

More presentations, from a court roll of 1531. There are some words not hitherto encountered in this book.

Line 1   The last word is *voc'*; note the little curled mark continuing the '*c*' indicating the abbreviation.

Line 2   *in capite* usually means 'as appears above the name'.

Line 3   Note *p<re>est*, an abbreviation of *preceptum est*; note also the gerunds after *ad* followed by an accusative object of the gerunds which are, you will remember, verbal nouns, and stating what the bailiff (dative case) has been ordered to do.

Line 4   A time limit has been set with a heavy penalty for non-compliance by the offender.

Line 6   Orders concerning Richard Messing's dog.

Line 7   The ninth word is *legio<rum>*; *d<omi>ni Regis*; *for<isfacturarum>*.

Example 9

Example 9
Again a difficult hand, from a court roll of Easter Week, 1552. The abbreviations in this document are also the subject of special treatment in Appendix C. Work hard at the transcription before you turn to the answer; it will pay off.

A new lord of the manor is holding his first court and receives the acknowledgement [*attornamentum*] of his tenants, whose names are listed.

Line 1   Note carefully the *'T'* of Thome, a letter occurring again; the two *'l'*s of Lovell are crossed unnecessarily; study the double looped *'A'* of *Armig<er>i*.

Line 6   Note the *'R'* of *Remyngton.*

Line 7-8   'All free and villein tenants and farmers'; *exacti fuerunt.*

Line 8   Note the tail of the *'q'* in *quibus* curling left rather than right, and the abbreviation mark for *-us.*

Line 9   The site of the manor house and the demesne land have been leased, an important point in the history of the manor. Do not forget the main aim – gathering material for local history research – in the excitement and challenge of transcription.

Line 11-12   *dur<ante> minor<e> etat<e>*

Line 12   *Se attornaverunt; p<re>fati*

Note the abbreviation *lib'; lib<er>* – free (i.e. freeholder) above some names. These are shown within round brackets in the answers.

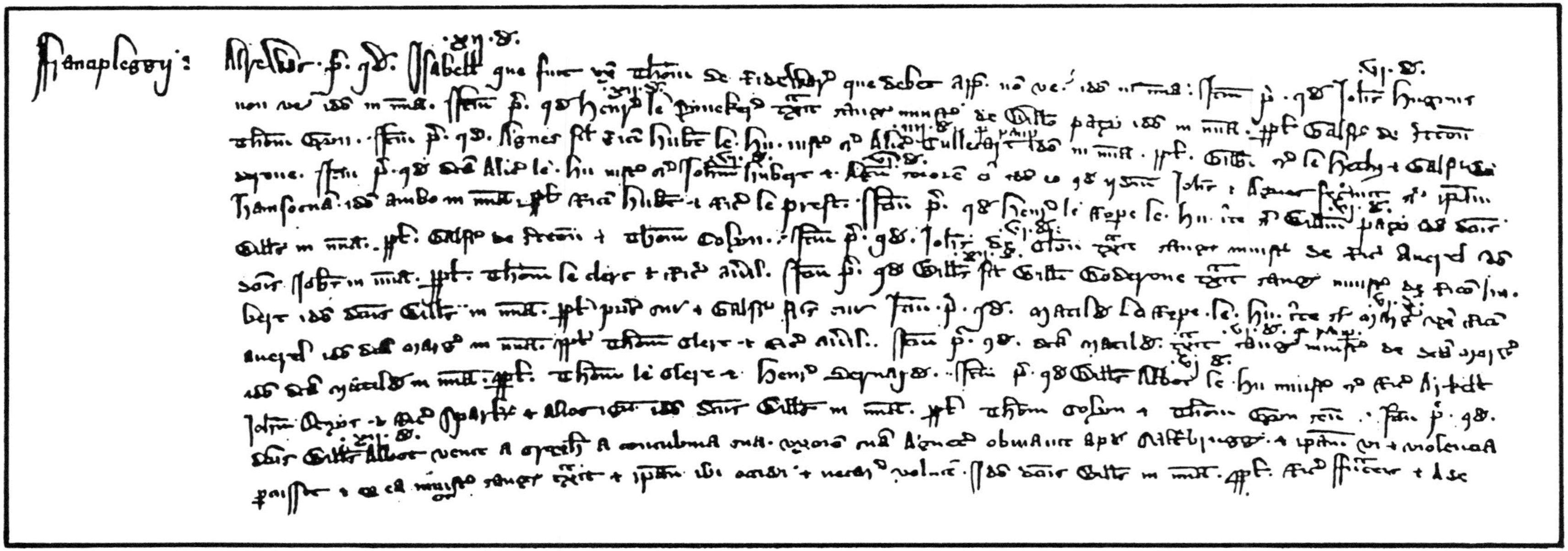

Example 10

Example 10
You may find this extract from a manor court roll of the mid-14th century the hardest yet to transcribe because of the small hand and the very abbreviated Latin. The frankpledges of Alrewas, Staffordshire, are making their presentments: the hue and cry has been raised several times, there is much violence with blood drawn, sex, and some useful local topographical detail. The notes diminish as you get used to the hand and repetitions occur.

Line 1   *p' q'd p<resentant> q<uo>d*; note how the amount of the fine imposed by the assessors is written over the names; *Isabell<a>*; *Ridewar<e>*; study the form of a terminal *'s'* as in *Joh<anne>s* and *hugonis*, which appears many times in this document; note also the way in which *id<e>o* is abbreviated.

Line 2   *t<ra>xit sang<uin>e<m>*; count the minims in the next word to make the Latin for *iuste* or *iniuste*; the tail of the *'y'* in *Paty* curls sharply round to touch the preceding letter; possibly *s<tre>tton*.

Line 3   *s<upe>r*; the words inserted are the amount of the fine followed by *q<uia> paup<er>*, i.e. the fine has been reduced because Alice is a pauper; the last letters in the line are part of a name *Goderone* which is completed in the next line; you will have noticed that where the hue and cry has been raised the fine is placed over the name of the offender, either the person who raised it or against whom it was raised.

Line 4   *sorore<m> ei<us>*

Line 5   'justly' – the Latin is very abbreviated; the last word in the line is *d<i>c<t>us*.

Line 7   last word is part of a name continued in the next line.

Line 11   *alios ign<otos>*

Line 12   probably *croxh<alt>*; *obivavit*, an unusual spelling.

Example 11

Example 11
This is from a court roll of a monastic manor of the late 14th century. It contains a few new words. The heading gives the abbot's year of office as well as the saint's day and the regnal year.

Line 3   Possibly *Pyp* or *Pyp<er>*; the clerk stands proxy for all the absentees.

Line 6   *sum<monitus>*

Line 7   He did not come so it was ordered that he be distrained *cont<ra> p<ro>x<imam>*; understand *curiam*

Line 8   *Wyghtmer<e>*

Line 9   *manupasti sui; mariol*

Line 10   *cul<pabilis> un<de> inqu<isit>io*

Line 11   The scribe's insertion above the line makes better sense at the end of this entry, where it is placed in the answers.

Line 14   The plaintiff is fined for failing to prosecute his suit against the defendant.

Line 16   *pull<u>m* foal

Example 12

Example 12

From the rolls of a manor court of 1636. Dating by saints' days has long since been abandoned. A fairly legible hand with one or two new words.

Line 1   *vicesimo septimo*

Line 9   'did not appear but made default'

Line 10   In fact the fines do not appear above their names.

Line 11   *panem*

Line 12   *cervic<iam>*

Line 13   The standard phrase is reduced to *I<de>o etc.*

Example 13

Example 13
From a late 17th-century court roll of a manor of the Duchy of Lancaster. The florid legal hand can cause difficulties. The business is restricted to copyhold transactions, and before you attempt the transcription read the earlier sections on this topic.

Line 2   The presence of customary tenants is recorded; this was a legal necessity.

Line 4   The scribe's initial flourish on the *'v'* of *vener<unt>* should be studied because the letter appears again.

Line 5   Note the flourish after the *'d'* of *p<re>d<icti>*.

Line 6   *Belmote Lane*

Line 8   As is often the case a following adjective may give a guide to the transcription of the endings of previous nouns: in this case *suo<rum>* will help with the previous words.

Line 12   The last letter in this line looks like a *'d'* but grammatically the word should be *consuetis,* agreeing with *redditibus* and *serviciis.*

Examples 14 and 15

Example 14

From the same manor and referring to the same tenements as in Example 13, but from a court of about two hundred years earlier. Compare the hands for yourself.

Line 1   *Jur<atores> ex offic<i>o videl<i>c<et>*

Line 4   Presentations may begin, as in this case, with 'The jurors present that ...' plus a new clause with a nominative subject, but another form found is 'The jurors present ...' plus an accusative object.

Line 5   Note the more usual spelling *nichil.*

Line 6   *heres*; extend *hereditizand'* into a gerundive agreeing with the nouns it refers to in the dative plural.

Line 9   Distinguish between *cons'*, a noun, to be extended, in this case, as *consuetudines* and the second *cons'* in the line to be extended as *consueta*, a past participle in the same case as 'rents, services and customs' which are direct objects of the gerund *reddendo* at the end of line eight.

Example 15

This extract is from a manor court roll of the mid-16th century. The jury of inquiry is reporting on under-age persons in the care of the king, non-attenders are fined, orders are issued concerning the maintenance of hedges and a butcher selling rotten meat is amerced.

Line 6   *tenent<iarius>* rather than the more usual *tenens.*

Line 7   Note the subjunctive *p<er>mittet*, used because the jury has made an order.

Line 9   What case and number the scribe had in mind after *quilib<e>t* is uncertain.

Line 13   The last three words are *ult<ra> o<mn>ia b<e>n<e>*; watch for various highly abbreviated forms of this phrase at the end of jury presentments.

Examples 16, 17 and 18

Example 16

This is in the flamboyant hand characteristic of the later Elizabethan and early Jacobean period. Note the words described as *Anglice*, i.e. 'in English'.

Line 1   The fourth word is *p<re>d<i>c<t>i*; last word *communem* agreeing with *p<ar>cum*.

Line 3   *insup<er>; sup<er>*

Line 4   'trespassed and each of them trespassed'

Line 5   *Ideoq<ue> ip<s>i et eor<um> quil<ibe>t*

Line 7   *decurrere*

Example 17

From a manor court roll of the reign of Edward III. The saint referred to in the dating is Sedde, i.e. Chad, bishop of Mercia.

Line 2   He surrenders 'a cottage'.

Line 3   *in ead<e>m*; note the difficult initial '*M*' of Matilda with its weak first minim and the elongation and curl of the third minim; note also the way that '*t*' and '*i*' are joined making them hard to discern as two letters.

Line 4   *dote*; note the superscript abbreviation mark ⁹ in *uni<us>*.

Line 5-6   Learn to recognise the phrase 'for services thence formerly owed'; usually 'and accustomed' is included.

Example 18

Extracts from this court roll of 1259 have already been provided in Examples 1(e) and 2(d). This extract adds new words and phrases in the same attractive but difficult hand. See also Appendix C.

Line 1   Note the superscript letter indicating omission of letters; as noted before the ascenders are bifurcated; you will recall also the sign ꝯ, its tail coming below the line and meaning, when it appears at the beginning of a word, *con-*. The case has been respited to the next court.

Line 2   Extend *dist<ri>n͞g* into a passive voice verb; *et et<iam>* – no, the scribe did not write *et* twice; this time the mark ⁹ is superscript, and the word is *q<uia>*.

Line 4   *Av<er>il*; he is in mercy for a complaint he has instituted – *mota*.

Line 7   Note the mark ȝ for *-et* in *scilic<et>*.

Chapter 2:
Rentals and Extents

Rentals usually list the names of tenants, the nature of their tenure, and the amount of rent each pays; occasionally they include a brief description of what tenants hold, there may be a formal mention of services due from each occupant, and sometimes these are particularised, in which case they are in effect also custumals (see later). Rentals are much less frequently found than manor court rolls, because by their nature they were compiled only occasionally, perhaps on the occasion of a new lord of the manor taking over. Where they have survived they are valuable additional sources of material for local history research. Some urban rentals give street names and where the manor covers the whole of the town or village it is possible to use rentals to reconstruct local topography and even to offer rough estimates of population size. Occasionally they provide descriptions of the properties listed. The nature of rentals renders them easy to understand, and abbreviations are so often repeated that transcription and extension present few problems.

Exercise 12: Translate

(a) *Rentale factum et renovatum per sacrum Johannis Blounte et Arturi Meverell xx<mo> Aprilis 1573 et anno regni domine nostre Elizabethe xv<to>*

A rental is often 'made and renewed', or some very similar phrase.

(b) *Willelmus filius Henrici Lug tenet tenementum quondam Willelmi avi sui solvendo vj denarios*

Holdings are often identified by reference to a previous holder in the genitive case.

(c) *Ricardus de Potlak carpentarius tenent unum burgagium de iure Elene uxoris sue solvendo abbati xijd.*

Rentals, particularly in towns, sometimes specify by what right the tenement is held: the lord might be able to raise rents of tenements not held by hereditary right more easily.

(d) *Johannes de London tenet unum cotagium et unam acram terre que reddere solebat per annum iijs.vjd. modo ijs.*

(e) *Alicia de Stafford tenet tenementa nuper Benedicti Mountgomery et reddit per annum termino Pentecostes iiijd. vel unam libram cimini*

It is unlikely the rent was still being paid in kind.

(f) *Radulphus Leysing nativus tenet unum messuagium et unam virgatam terre nuper Ricardi Leysing et reddit per annum terminis Martini et Nativitatis Iohannis Baptiste iijs.vjd.*

Note the term used for a villein, serf or bond tenant. Medieval rents were usually paid in two, or four, but not necessarily in equal, instalments. Here the tenant holds this tenement by a money rent and is obviously rising out of the ranks of the mere serfs. His servile obligations for other tenements still obtain, but these, of which two are listed in the next entries, have also been commuted to a money rent.

(g) *Idem Radulphus debet falcare in pratis domini per unum diem sumptibus suis propriis et dat pro eodem opere iiijd.*

'at his own expenses' i.e. his food and drink are not supplied by the lord when he works on the demesne meadows.

(h) *... et levabit fenum per annum diem ... et metet in autumpno per iij dies ... et arrabit per unum diem ad semen yemale et ad semen quadragesimale ...*

Note the use of the future tense; 'winter' and 'spring'.

Extension of Abbreviations in Rentals

Exercise 13: Transcribe, extending the abbreviations within brackets, and translate.

(a) *Ad' de Neuton' t3 burg' qᵒ ndā Johēs Penifot de iur' Marg'ie ux' sue solv' iiijd.*

Note the extreme form of abbreviation of *t<enet>* by means of the mark rather like a cursive 'z' i.e. ₃ . The other abbreviation marks like apostrophes, superscript letters, and straight lines over parts of a word, are standard.

(b) *Johēs Lugg ten' di' acr' t're arabilis et redd' ꝑ annꝰ xvjd.*

Note that the usual form is 'a half acre' not 'half an acre' and that therefore *di'* must be extended as an adjective agreeing with its noun. All the abbreviation marks have been previously encountered.

(c) *Witts le Park' t' un' mess' cꝰ ptm̄ redd' e' t' xxd.*

e<isdem> t<erminis> are the only new words in this entry and refer to terms, i.e. dates for payment of rent, previously mentioned in the rental.

(d) *Dn̄s Thō de Aldelꝰ capell's t3 ad t'm vite sue un' acr' et di' et redd' vjd.*

Priests were usually given the honorary title of *Dominus* 'Sir': ensure your extension of *un'* agrees with the noun it is qualifying; this time *di'* could be *dimidium* as a noun in its own right.

(e) *Alic' fil' Radi Baron ten' al' di' dc̄i ten' de dono patr' sui et reddit vjd.*

alterum dimidium; you must distinguish between the possible extensions of *al'*, which could be the abbreviation of *alius* or *alter*.

(f) *Galf' pist' t₃ q⁴md' plac' q° nd' J' frīs sui*

Terms in rentals are often severely abbreviated, as in this example. Be careful to distinguish *quidam* in its various cases and genders from *quondam* when you encounter them in abbreviated forms.

(g) *Elena fil' Walt'ᵢ tinctor' tenet un' parcell' prati iuxta Skyrem' medwe et extendit se ex t' v'so ad alt' viam*

Rentals often give locations helpful in reconstructing the lay-out of an area; the spelling *medwe* is often found; *se* in *extendit se* need not be translated; note the superscript abbreviation for *-ra* in 'across'.

Examples 19 and 20

Example 19
This is an extract from a rental of 1544 which was a borough – hence the burgage rents – but had never evolved as such.

Line 1   Do not be misled by the line fillers which are linked to the brackets.

Line 2   Note the extra downward stroke of the *'p'* in the scribe's abbreviation of
          p<er>tin<enciis>; the Roman numeral *'x'* in this hand looks like a *'p'*.

Line 3   *Solvend<o> ad f<estu>m*

Line 6   Again the scribe has crossed out some words; *sol<vendo> eod t<erm>ino*.

Line 9   Note the abbreviation for *-us* in *duob<us>* where the scribe has used what is a
          dative or ablative form when grammatically one would have expected an
          accusative *duos*.

Example 20
From the same rental as in the previous example. Whereas the free tenants are holding
burgages the copyholders have messuages and the rents are considerably higher.

Line 3   The surname is *Harvye*, it appears again in line seven.

Example 21

Example 21
A final extract from this rental which lists tenants of demesne lands.

Line 1   *cert<as> p<ar>cell<as>*

Possibly you had trouble with this hand, but the repetition of words and phrases should have helped. With this extract, as with all the others, do not struggle too long before looking at the answers, but if you do fail it is important to attempt the transcriptions again after a day or so.

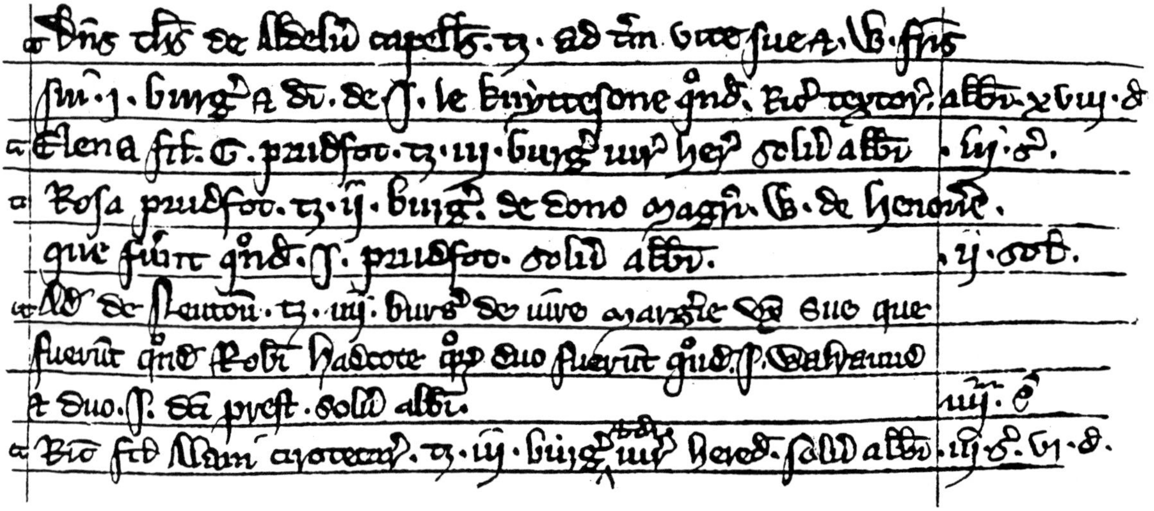

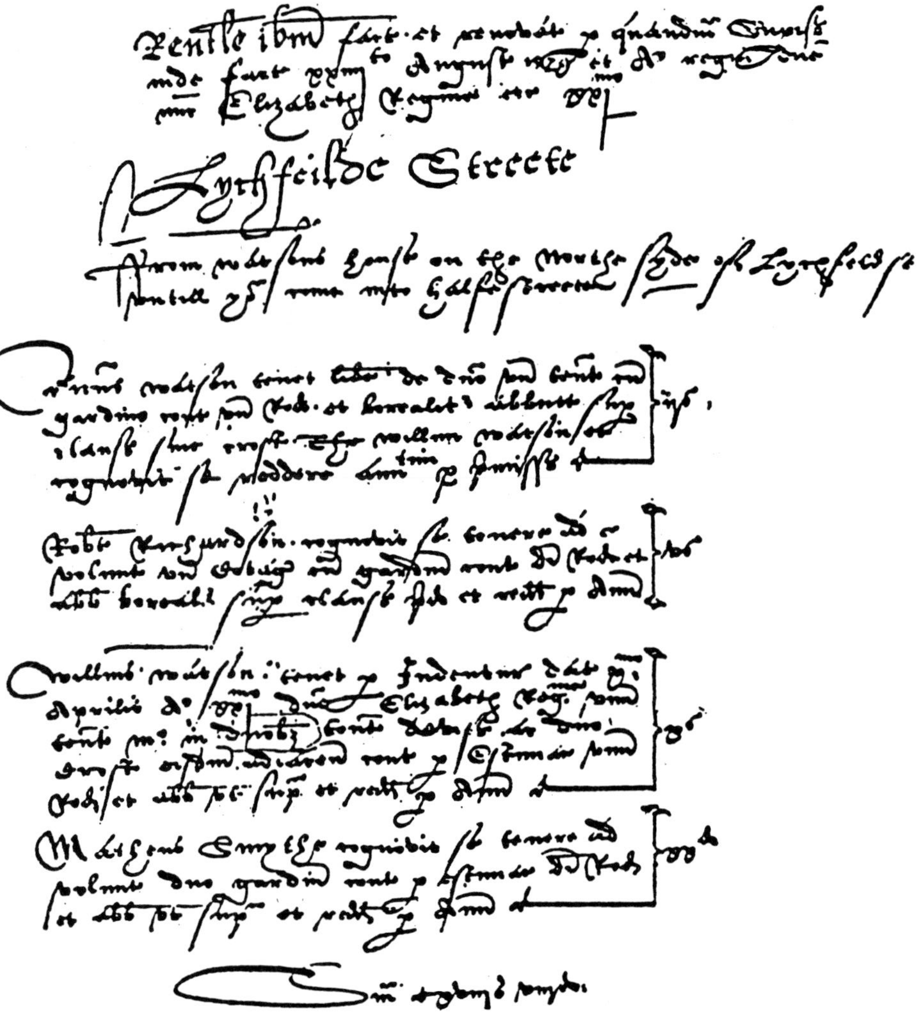

Examples 22 and 23

Example 22

This is from a rental of a monastic borough in 1319. The compiler is careful to state by what right a tenement is held. Some trades found in the borough at the time are shown. The normal rent for a burgage tenement in this borough was 12d. a year. The hand is easy to read. Watch the letter 't' which appears almost like a capital 'T' but in a lower case form. The capital 'W' as it appears in the manuscripts of the early 14th century is at first difficult. If you are in real trouble look at the transcription of the first line in the answers right away. As soon as you get used to the hand you will find it fairly easy to read, there is so much repetition.

Line 1   *Aldelu<m>*, i.e. the modern Audlem in Cheshire; Thomas is a chaplain hence the honorary title 'Dominus'.

Line 2   *q<uo>nd<am>* may be translated 'formerly belonging to'; *textor<is>*; the scribe has omitted the gerund *solvendo* in this line, presumably because he was squeezed for space.

Line 3   *iur<e> her<editario>*

Line 4   *mag<ist>ri; Henove<r>*, the modern Heanor in Derbyshire.

Line 7   'of which two formerly belonged to'

Line 9   Richard is the son of Alan the glover.

Example 23

From a rental of 1579. Note the mixture of English with the Latin.

Line 1   Rentals are nearly always 'made and renewed'; the last word could be *sup<er>vis<ionem>* or possibly *sup<er>vis<um>*.

Line 7   *ten<emen>t<um>*

Line 8   The location of a tenement is often defined by reference to compass points and adjoining tenements; *borealit<er>*; take care to extend *abbutt'* correctly.

Line 9   The final letter of the first word presents difficulty for extension, because one would normally have an accusative case after *super*.

Line 16   *m<od>o*

Line 17   The scribe appears to have had *unum* in mind but grammatically *unam* is required to agree with *Rod<am>*.

Example 24

Example 24

From a manor court roll of the early 15th century. Not an easy hand.

Line 1   This time the rental is *renovatu<m> et factu<m>* by two inhabitants who were 'then collectors'.

Line 2   *coram; Sudb<er>y; t<un>c*

Line 3   Note how the two *'q'*s bend to the left like a *'g'*.

Line 4   Note the extreme abbreviation of *r<eddendo> p<er> a<nnum>*.

Line 6   Abbreviations again at the end of the line. The last two words are *e<isdem> t<erminis>*; watch for repeats in the next lines.

Line 7   Bagot was the lord of a neighbouring manor.

Line 8   *Isold<a> Ha<r>v<e>y*

Line 9   There is often some difficulty in deciding which preceding noun the past participle *voc'* is agreeing with; in this case it is reasonably clear that the agreement is with *t<er>r<e>*.

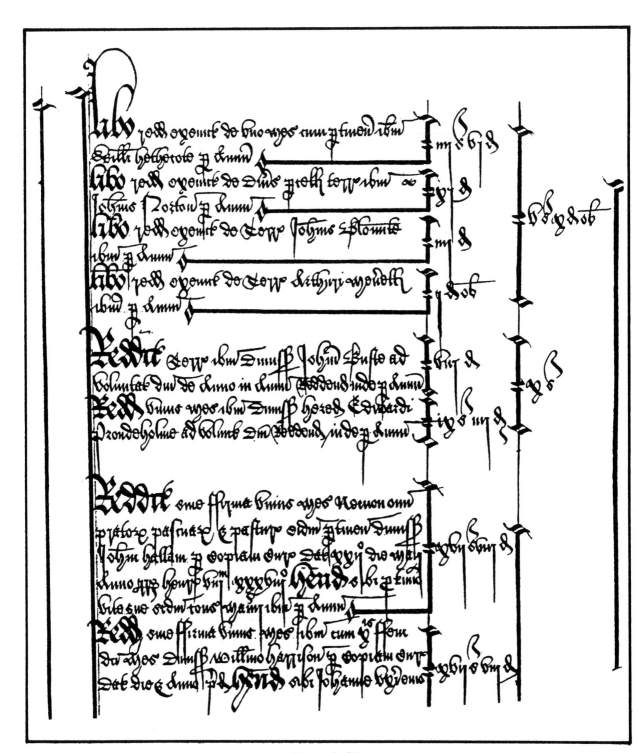

Example 25

Example 25

From a rental of 1546, written in a beautiful hand. See also a detailed treatment of the abbreviations in this document in Appendix C.

Line 1   *Lib<erati>o*, meaning 'payment', but with only a faint abbreviation mark; extend the next two words into the genitive case, and also in the same constructions in the following lines. The reading *Lib<eri> redd<itus> exeunt<es>* seems unlikely.

Line 5   *Blounte*

Line 7   *Meverell*, the stroke after the final *'l'* being only a flourish.

Line 9   'demised'; ensure in your transcription that the past participle agrees with the noun it refers to.

Line 10   Extend *reddend'* as an ablative gerund, and similarly in line 12.

Line 14   The scribe has carefully distinguished between *prato<rum>*, *pascua<rum>* and *pastur<e>*.

Line 18   penultimate word is *(xis)* [*decimis*], i.e. tenths or tithes.

Example 26

Extents

The extent is a survey in which all the manorial property – land, buildings, labour services, rents paid in kind – is valued, value being defined as its potential annual rent. Sometimes the extent follows a standard format, valuing the manor house, then the arable demesne land, meadow, etc. and ending with valuations of the tenants' rents and labour services.

Extents declined in number after the middle of the 14th century when demesne farming diminished as a consequence of the Black Death.

Example 26

This is fairly typical of this type of document. It begins with the title of the manor, the date, and the names of the persons on whose evidence, made on oath, the extent has been compiled. It then goes on to detailed valuations.

The handwriting displays the characteristics of the late 13th century and is not at all easy to read although it is attractive to look at: heavy strokes of the pen alternate with lighter strokes, the ascenders bifurcate at the top, the *'d'* bends well over to the left with a loop, the abbreviation marks over the letters are thick. Study particularly the *'a'* in such words as Maynard in line three; *'s'* and *'t'* together as in *pastur<a>* in line eight needs care. Do persevere with this document, referring at first to the answer for each word if necessary, until you can read the letters; many manorial records are found with this style of handwriting at this period.

Line 1	*Brytheston;* 'extent of the manor of the priory of Okeborn made'; note the *'N'* of *Nativitat<is>*.
Lines 2-3	Names of jurors; ninth word is *Stiward*; it is useful to consult an alphabet for initial capital letters.
Line 3	*qui dic<unt> q<uo>d; Cur<ia>* is 'house'.
Line	*val<et>; s<er>vic<ia> <e>t op<er>at<iones>*
Line 5	Last word is *vo-* and is continued in the next line to make *voluntate*.
Line 6	*p<er>quis<ita>* is a nominative neuter plural; sometimes when this word is used to mean profits of the court *perquisitum* is preferred.
Line 8	There is a paragraph mark before the word *Summa* (note the *'S'* again) and the final total.

Chapter 3:
Manorial Accounts

Manorial accounts are not always distinct from rentals. The former, called *compoti*, emerged in the early 13th century as an increasing number of lords of the manor used local officials to manage their demesnes. Accounts often provide not only statements of income and expenditure but much detail on the economic working of the manor. A full discussion of the development and format of manorial accounts is provided by Harvey, *op. cit.*, chapter III, which should be used as necessary to supplement the following brief treatment.

Exercise 14: Translate

(a) *Radulphus prepositus de Barton reddit compotum de viij li xijd obolum a crastino sancti Michaelis*

The account normally opens with the name and title of the official, often the bailiff *ballivus*, sometimes the reeve *prepositus*, then the dates covered. Figures are in Roman numerals; *libras* is left abbreviated in the transcription above; note 'halfpenny'.

(b) *Compotus Willelmi Clapbroke prepositi ibidem a festo sancti Michaelis anno tertio Regis Edwardi quarti usque idem festum sancti Michaelis tunc proximum anno eiusdem Regis quarti scilicet per unum annum integrum*

Note the change in the usual position of the ordinal indicating the regnal year.

(c) *Et de vj li. vs. vd. de redditu assise de termino Annunicationis*

'Fixed rents' are often distinguished from other types.

(d) *Idem reddit compotum de xxjs.viijd. de operationibus et consuetudinibus venditis*

Day works and customs have been 'sold', i.e. commuted to money payments and these must be accounted for.

(e) *Exitus manerii. Idem reddit compotum de ijs.vd. redditus de pannagio porcorum tenentium domini ... et de vs. redditus de viij gallis et vj gallinis venditis*

'Issues of the manor', i.e. profits or revenues; the original extract contains many more items produced in the manor. You may find that spellings vary from those in the dictionary.

(f) *Firma piscarii Et de xiijs. de firma piscarii aque de Foxford*

(g) *Perquisitiones curie. Et de ixs.vijd. de perquisitionibus duorum visuum ibidem tentorum*

Profits of courts of view of frankpledge could include fines for breaking the assizes of bread and ale, for default of attendance, trespasses etc.

(h) *Summa totalis receptorum cum arreragiis xlj li. ixs.vd. quart<am>*

Abbreviations in manorial accounts can cause difficulty until the vocabulary is familiar. Abbreviations of words already used in the exercises above include *comp<otus>*; *r<edditus>*; *vend<itus/a/um>*; *exit<us>*; *arrer<agia>*. Many more are found in the following examples.

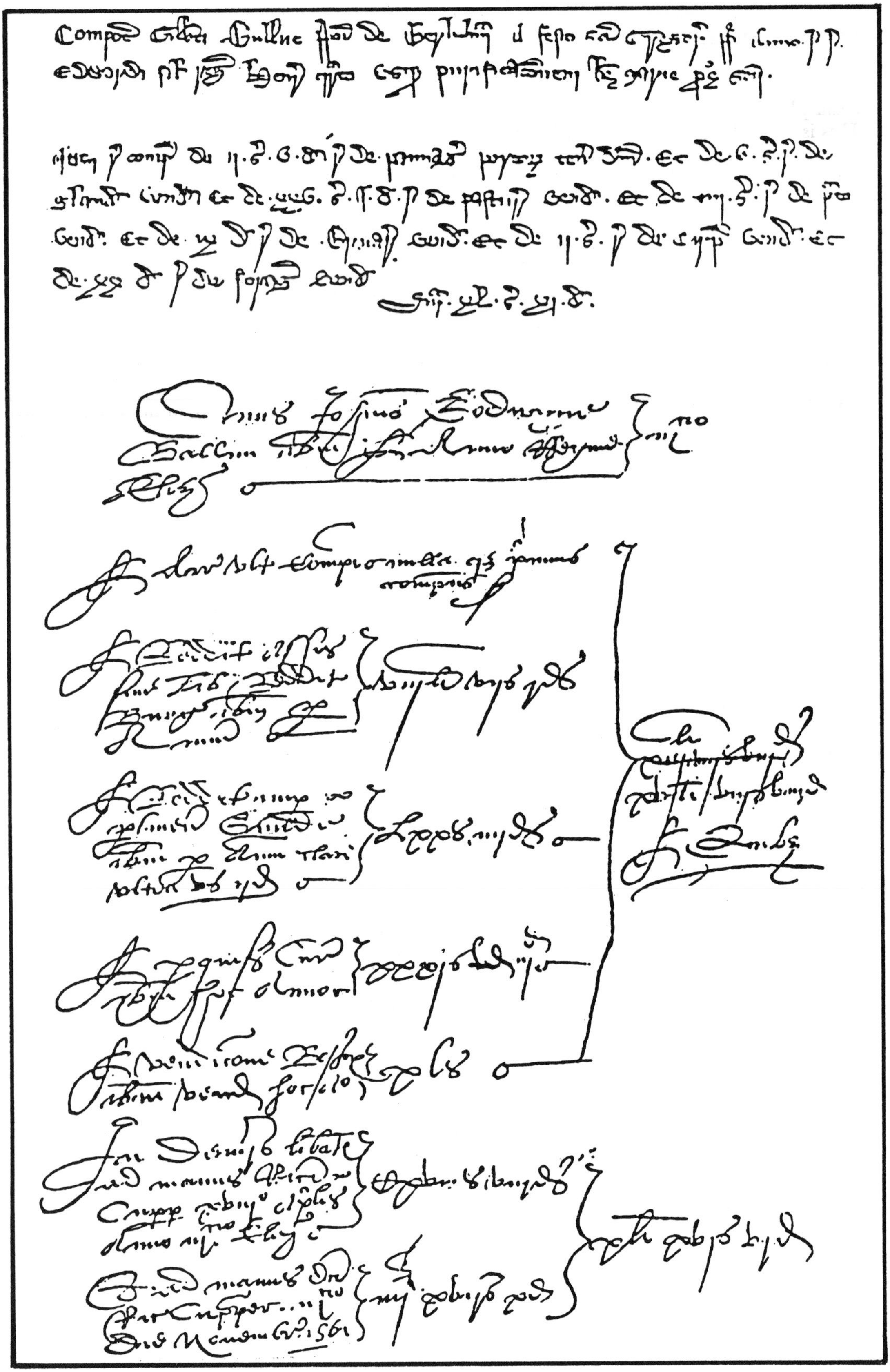

Examples 27, 28 and 29

Example 27
This is in a difficult 13th-century hand.

Line 1   *Bulluc*, he is the reeve of Berlinham; *Gregor<ii>*

Line 2   *Henr<ici> q<ua>rto*, note the form of the '*q*' and in the following word *usq<ue>*; note also the general mark of abbreviation indicating in this case *-ue*, as usual the '*i*' is omitted from the combination of letters *-ion*.

Example 28
From the same document and containing some new words.

Line 1   Item; the single letter '*r*' appears twice in this line, first as an abbreviation for *r<eddit>* and then as an abbreviation for *r<eceptis>*, a past participle agreeing with *v s<olidis>* which is ablative plural after *de*.

Line 2   *gland<iis> vend<itis>*; last word *p<ra>to*

Line 3   *bruar<iis>*, but the word could be spelt in a number of ways; *sirp<is>* is without the '*c*' with which it is usually spelt.

Example 29
A sprawling 'secretary' hand of the mid-16th century, difficult to read. There are some new words to add to the vocabulary of accounts, and there is some useful practice in transcribing Roman numerals.

Line 1   *Onus*

Line 2   A complex '*R*' in *Regine*.

Line 4   Probably the first word is *de*, 'for'; *arreragiis q<uia>*.

Line 6   *sive*, learn to recognise the final '*e*', often quickly and carelessly written in the 16th century.

Line 10   *p<er>tinen<tis>* here a present participle in the ablative plural, from *pertineo*, easy to confuse with *pertinentiis*; *Guilde* the manor had previously belonged to Burton Abbey and a religious gild held land in the manor.

Line 11   *clare* i.e. nett.

Line 14   part of the total is crossed through.

Line 15   'sale of wood'

Line 17   'monies delivered'

Chapter 4:
Custumals

The custumal was a survey of rents, services and other customary obligations owed by tenants, both free and unfree, to the lord of the manor, and of the rights and obligations of the lord. Sometimes these obligations were basically uniform, with only slight minor variations, for all the tenants in one class; more often they varied from individual to individual. Custumals exist in less-developed form from the early 12th century but became more comprehensive in time. By the 14th century they had begun to decline and there are few custumals dated after the Black Death. In some manors custumals were not committed to writing but rested on oral testimony.

Custumals are not necessarily to be taken at face value as a record of labour services or other obligations. They represent a legal and theoretical record of the lord's and tenants' rights and obligations rather than an actual one. In the course of time services or produce owed were often commuted to money payments. Custumals should be used in conjunction with other manorial records to obtain a more reliable picture of the local medieval scene.

No two manors were exactly similar in the obligations and services exacted by the lord. In the early medieval period free tenants, i.e. who paid rents, were not entirely relieved of manorial duties or agricultural services such as lending ploughs or doing fence work. Villeins had so many obligations that one wonders how they found time to till their own lands.

Translation

The vocabulary of custumals includes words often not encountered elsewhere. The following exercises provide a short selection of the many words and terms that may be found.

Exercise 15: Translate

(a) *Willelmus de Sobehalle tenet ij bovatas pro ij solidis et debet ire ubicumque mittitur*

From an early 12th-century document, showing commutation to a money rent combined with an indefinite service obligation.

(b) *Tintor habet ij bovatas pro ij solidis et vj denariis et debet bis in anno prestare aratrum suum et ter in Augusto secare duabus vicibus cum j homine tercia cum omnibus suis ad cibum domini*

'The dyer' is obviously a substantial tenant and the manorial tenants are already economically differentiated; the lord provides food at harvest time.

(c) *Quisque villanus tenet ij bovatas et operatur ij diebus in hebdomeda ... et debet ij gallinas ad natale ... et dat pasnagium et bis arat in anno et preter hoc in Quadragesima dimidiam acram et a Pentecosta usque ad festum omnium sanctorum mittit animalia sua in faldam domini*

This 12th-century document uses a classical deponent verb *operor* where later medieval usage allows *opero; natale <Christi>*; note the variant of *pannagium.*

(d) *Idem faciet diversa averagia et cariagia de victualibus et aliis necessariis domini quandocumque premunitus fuerit et dat pro eodem opere per annum ijs.xd.*

Note the use of the future tense and of the future perfect. The open-ended obligations of carrying services have been commuted to a fairly heavy sum.

(e) *... et debet talliari quolibet anno cum vicinis suis ad festum sancti Martini*

Abbreviations in custumals differ little from those in rentals, and tend to be fewer because custumals were not so often written or revised. Vocabulary apart, they are in general easier to read than other types of manorial record.

Exercise 16: Transcribe, extending the abbreviations, and then translate.

(a) *Et q'libet septimana opabili a p'dc̄o festo usq' ad festw̄ s̄c̄i Pet' ad vinctā debet opari p t's dies q̄lc̄ūq̄' d̄n̄s voluerit*

'week of works'

(b) *Et avrare debet p unā dietā et quiet' es' de ij opib₃*

'day's journey'

(c) *Et si equw̄ vendid'it inf' man'iw̄ v'l ext' ex's Nundinis dabit ad theolon' ijd.*

v<e>l often looks like *ut; extra; exceptis*.

(d) *Idē d₃ met'e in autūpno v₃ uno die cw̄ uno hoīe sc̄d̄o die cw̄ duob₃ hōīb₃ s̄n̄ cibo*

Note the general abbreviation mark ₃ used four times in this entry, with different significance; *s<i>n<e>*.

(e) *...t'io die duos hoīes ad magnw̄ metebene et erit custos eoɤ tota die*

'boon-reaping'; he (the tenant) will be responsible for their food, an obligation which frequently appears in custumals.

(f) *Idē d₃ arare bis in yeme et semel in quadrages'*

(g) *It' equw̄ no' deb₃ vende' s̄n̄ lic' d̄n̄i*

The words are severely abbreviated; the prohibition concerning horses is frequently found.

(h) *Idē deb₃ merchet pro filia sua maritanda ad vol' d̄n̄i*

One of the usual servile obligations.

The following extracts are from a monastic custumal of the early 14th century. They list the obligations of John le Bond, a *nativus* of Burton Abbey, who held a virgate of land. The commutation of his labour services was already proceeding, for apparently he did no regular weekly work [*opera*] on the lord's demesne but paid 2s. a year rent. However, he still had to perform various seasonal services including hay-making with one or two men, reaping, ploughing in Lent and winter and carting wood. Some lines from this manuscript have already been transcribed in Exercise 16.

The first few lines of the manuscript show many of the characteristics of the handwriting of the period; some ascenders are bifurcated, for instance, the '*l*' in *solvit* in line one and in *levandum* in line three; the '*t*' is crossed low down and can be mistaken sometimes for '*c*'; the ascender of the '*d*' curls back to touch the loop, as in *bonde* and *ad*; the main abbreviation marks are the superior florid comma-like sign as in *t<er>min<um>* and the bold horizontal stroke, e.g. *annuati<m>* in line one and *ho<m>i<n>em* in line three; the scribe normally uses a double-looped '*a*' though not invariably; note how the scribe forms an initial '*m*', the first minim curled, the last extended.

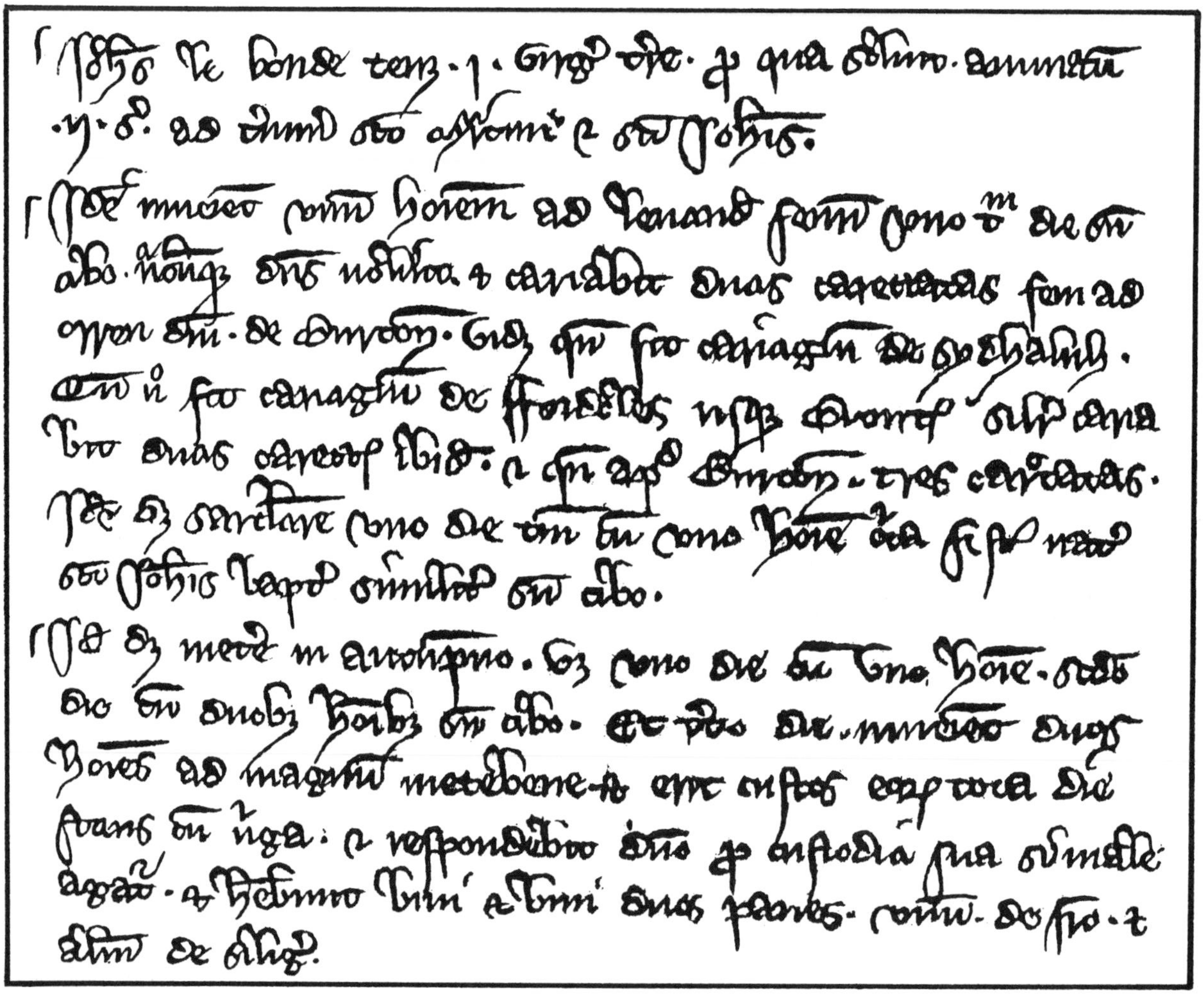

Example 30

Example 30

Line 1   'holds 1 virgate of land'; last word *annuati\<m>*

Line 2   Note how the same abbreviation mark serves twice in *t\<er>m\<i>n\<os>*.

Line 3   The scribe uses a future tense *inve\<n>iet.*

Line 4   The first two words are *cibo q\<ua>cumq\<ue>*; study the letters in *voluit,* noting that the scribe uses a future perfect tense.

Line 5-6   *orreu\<m>*; always try an *'h'* in front of an *'o'*; *sydhaluh* possible *scindula,* 'shingles'.

Line 6   *Fordeles* possible 'fardels', cf. Hamlet, III, i, 76. The end of the last word in this line is in the next line.

Line 13   The idea is that he is responsible for seeing that they do not work badly.

Line 14   The first word is *agat\<ur>* which uses the usual abbreviation mark for the passive voice form ending in *-ur.*

The following extract is from a long custumal of the mid-13th century. In this document, as in most custumals, look for a series of infinitive verbs depending on *debet* which concern farming tasks such as sowing, reaping, harrowing and carting. You may find it difficult because of the small handwriting, the many abbreviations and the technical vocabulary. If necessary use the transcription in the answers immediately, even for every word, until you begin to recognise the letters more easily and are able to do much more on your own. This is the final example in the book, and it is as hard as you are likely to meet in the course of your own local history research. If you can do this, even if many mistakes and omissions are made initially, you can do most documents.

Example 31

Example 31

Line 1   *et qu<ando>; op<er>at<ur>*

Line 2   'in any week of works'; *p<er> t<res>; q<ua>l<e>cu<n>q<ue>*

Line 3   Note the verb for 'threshes' *t<ri>turat* and the rather unusual Latin word for 'strike'; *n<isi>*.

Line 5   *xl<a>* is an abbreviation for *quadragesima*; also found in line 13.

Line 6   *duc<er>e, locu<m>*

Line 7   *es<se>; quiet<us>*

Line 8   *q<ua>rt<erium> brasii* possibly meaning 'barley' rather than 'malt' as it still has to be dried.

Line 9   *tu<n>c*

Line 10   *op<er>e*

Answers to Exercises and Examples

In order to help beginners, translations are sometimes more literal than good English usage requires. Punctuation and capitalisation have been added only where necessary for clarity. In the transcriptions, extensions of abbreviated or contracted words and superscript letters in the originals, and any other editorial insertions, are enclosed within brackets. In making the extensions classical Latin usage has been followed. Occasionally more than one extension is possible, especially because 'c' and 't' are not always distinguishable, e.g. s<an>c<t>i and s<anc>ti. Where an accurate transcription is not possible because of damage to or fading of the original manuscript, or because of the scribe's hasty handwriting, the word is followed by a question mark in brackets or by three dots thus ... The apostrophe comma often found at the end of place-names, for example *Neuton'*, has been omitted in the transcriptions. Place-names have only been modernised in the translations where identification is certain.

Exercise 1 (p. 5)
(a) Tuesday 20 March 1347.
(b) Wednesday 6 October 1518.
(c) Monday 23 July 1330.
(d) Saturday 18 October 1393.

Exercise 2 (p. 5)
(a) Court held at ABC on Thursday next after the feast of Saint Barnabas the Apostle [15 June] in the year of our lord 1273.
(b) Small court held there on 3rd day of November in the 27th year of the reign of Henry VIII, by the grace of God of England, France and Ireland, king, defender of the faith and on earth supreme head of the English and Irish church [1535].
(c) View of frankpledge with court held on Thursday next after the feast of the Finding of the Holy Cross [6 May] in the 38th year of the reign of Henry VIII [1546].
(d) Court Baron of William Pargiter, gentleman, farmer of the aforesaid prebend, held at ABC.
(e) Small court of Humphrey Tyndall, clerk, Doctor of Sacred Theology, held before John Martin, gentleman, steward there.
(f) Court and Leet held there on Monday next after the feast of Saint Lucy the Virgin [18 December] in the 14th year of the reign of King Edward [1340].

Exercise 3 (p. 6)
(a) Henry the Southerner essoins himself by Robert son of Hod of common suit [of court], 1st [time].
(b) Robert the baker essoined himself by Richard the clerk of suit of court, 1st [time].
(c) William Adam essoined himself by Hugo the hayward of the same, [suit of court] 2nd [time].
(d) William Fox essoined himself by William Owen against Margery his sister in a plea of land, 1st [time]. Pledges of the said Margery for proceeding with her suit are Robert son of Ralph and Nicholas son of Ralph.
(e) William Docerill for [his non] appearance by William Croket, 1st [time].

71

Exercise 4 (p. 7)

(a) John Kemster complains of Agnes of Ragleye in a plea that she occupied a house and yard [curtilage] against [his] will, to [his] damage 40d. There was an inquiry and the jurors say that [she is] not guilty. Therefore he is in mercy.

(b) Adam Hichen complains of Henry Bust, frankpledge, in a plea that he unjustly presented against him that he [Adam] should repair one ditch when other tenants of the vill ought to repair [it].

(c) The abbot through his attorney is plaintiff against Robert the halswain in a plea of trespass. He [Robert] has not come therefore he is distrained.

(d) Richard Rond appears against Henry of Willington and Alice his wife. They do not appear and [their] pledge has defaulted therefore [let him] be better distrained.

(e) William Charle [is] plaintiff against Robert the laster in a plea of debt. Pledges for prosecuting [are] John Hobbeson and Adam his brother.

(f) Nicholas the comber seeks judgment against John of Stapenhill in a plea of trespass. It is decided that the said Nicholas may have a day.

Exercise 5 (p. 8)

(a) The frankpledges of Branston present that Alana wife of Robert Cuge sold ale contrary to the assize therefore [she is] in mercy.

(b) The same present that Henry the cartwright brewed contrary to the assize therefore [he is] in mercy.

(c) The frankpledges of Horninglow present that William, son of Radulph Ernald, who owes suit [of court] has not come.

(d) The frankpledges of Burton present that they know nothing.

(e) The 12 jurors present that Hugh (6d.) de Menill and Robert (6d.) his son unjustly drew blood from Robert of Gresley. They were attached and found pledges John of Bursincot and John of Stapenhill. Therefore etc.

(f) Likewise the hue and cry was raised against them justly, therefore [they are] in mercy by the same pledges.

(g) Likewise the inquiry between the household of Henry of Fold and Alice, the wife of William Orme, namely, concerning the raising of the hue and cry, is respited to next Saturday.

(h) Geoffrey of Monte is charged with destroying the pasture of [his] neighbours with 'foreign' animals.

Exercise 6 (p. 10)

(a) To this court came Edward Breerton of Morrey within the manor of ABCD aforesaid and Anne Breerton his wife, in their own persons, and before Zacharia Babington, gentleman, the aforesaid steward, claim to hold title to a certain meadow called Dan Meadow.

(b) And upon this into the same court came the aforesaid James Wright and Elizabeth Wright in their own persons and received from the lord of the manor the aforesaid premises [and] to them the lord by his steward aforesaid granted thence seisin by the rod according to the custom of the manor aforesaid.

(c) ... [that] neither Edward, Anne or Elizabeth themselves, nor their heirs, nor any one of them nor anyone else in their name or of any one of them any right, title, interest or claim in the aforesaid meadow for the future may demand or claim, but they shall be excluded from all legal action or claim.

(d)   ... to have and to hold the aforesaid premises to John Illsley [and] his heirs and assigns
at the will of the lord according to the custom of the manor aforesaid for the rents,
repairs and all other services thence formerly owed and by right accustomed, and at the
death of the aforesaid John Illsley the best animal or ox for a heriot, or £3, at the choice
of the lord of the aforesaid manor, and he gives to the lord at his entry £15 and he did
fealty and was admitted thence tenant on the aforesaid terms.

Exercise 7 (p. 12)

(a)   *Q<uo>d Ph<illipus> pistor deb<et> ixs.vjd. Ric<ardo> Meysey It deb<et> iijs.vjd. Matheo de
Lodelowe, It. d<ebet> d<omi>no ijs.vjd. q<ua>r<e> adjudicat<us> est ad carcere<m>
quousq<ue> solvit totu<m> vel inven<er>it pleg<ios>*

(b)   *Edit<ha> q<ue> fuit ux<or> Henr<ici> recup<er>at de debito suo viijs.jd. de Joh<ann>e Karles ad
solvend<um> in festo b<eat>i Michael<is>*

(c)   *M<emoran>d<um> q<uo>d Joh<ann>es de Stretton cl<er>icus ve<nit> i<n> plena cur<ia> et
fec<it> fidelitate<m> p<ro> q<ua>da<m> acr<a> t<er>re arab<i>lis q<uo>d habu<it> de
Ric<ardo> de Stretton*

Exercise 8 (p. 13)

(a)   *Vis<us> franc<iplegii> cu<m> cur<ia> tent<us> ib<ide>m die Jovis p<ro>x<ima> post fest<um>
Invent<i>o<n>is s<an>c<t>e cruc<is> anno regni reg<is> Henr<ici> octavi xxj°*

View of frankpledge with court held there on Thursday next after the feast of the Finding of
the Holy Cross [6 May 1529] in the 21st year of the reign of King Henry VIII.

(b)   *Cur<ia> man<er>ij p<re>d<ic>ti tent<a> ib<ide>m die Sab<bat>i p<ro>x<ima> ante fest<um>
s<an>c<t>i Mathei in estate anno r<egni> r<egis> Henrici sept<im>i post conq<uestu>m Anglie
sextodecimo*

Court of the aforesaid manor held there on Saturday next before the feast of Saint Matthew
in Summer [19 September 1500] in the 16th year of the reign of King Henry VII after the
conquest of England.

(c)   *Cur<ia> Baron<is> Philippi Pargiter Ar<migeri> ib<ide>m tent<a> p<ro> man<er>io
p<re>d<icto> anno regni d<omi>ni n<ost>ri Caroli s<e>c<un>di nunc Regis Anglie etc. xxxvj°
cor<am> D. Beech Sen<escallo>*

Court Baron of Philip Pargiter Esquire held there for the aforesaid manor in the 36th year of
the reign of our lord Charles 2nd 1684 now king of England etc. before D. Beech, steward.

Exercise 9 (p. 13)

(a)   *Rob<ertus> pistor ess<oniat> se p<er> Ric<ardu>m cl<er>icu<m> de secta cur<ie> p<ri>mo*

Robert the baker essoins himself by Richard the clerk of suit of court, 1st [time].

(b)   *Margareta Hynckley deb<et> sect<am> huius cur<ie> et fecit se essoniari*

Margaret Hynckley owes suit of this court and made [her] essoin.

(c) *Esson<ia>. Henr<icus> se de co<mmun>i p<er> Mauriciu<m> filiu<m> suu<m>. Rad<ulphu>s Wyllok se de eod p<er> Ad<am> Skipp<er>*

Essoins. Henry [essoins] himself of common [suit of court] by Maurice his son. Ralph Wyllock [essoins] himself of the same by Adam Skipper.

(d) *Will<elmu>s Fox esson<iat> se p<er> Will<elmu>m Owen v<ersu>s Margeriam soror de p<laci>to terre j°*

William Fox essoins himself by William Owen against Margery [his] sister in a plea of land, 1st [time].

Exercise 10 (p. 14)

(a) *Thomas Halley dec<ennarius> ib<ide>m present<at> Antoniu<m> Grey ijd. et Rob<er>tu<m> Grey p<ro> def<ec>tu apparant<ie> I<de>o quilib<e>t eo<rum> in m<isericord>ia d<omi>ni Et eleg<unt> in officio dec<ennarii> Joh<ann>em Sale Jur<atus>*

Thomas Halley tithingman there presents Antony Grey 2d. and Robert Grey for default of appearance. Therefore each of them [is] in the mercy of the lord. And they elect John Sale in the office of tithingman [and he is] sworn.

(b) *It<e>m p<re>sent<at> q<uo>d Ric<ard>us Porter (ijd.) fec<it> affraiam sup<er> Johannem Cartwright contra pacem etc. I<de>o ip<s>e in m<isericord>ia*

Likewise he presents that Richard Porter (2d.) assaulted John Cartwright against the peace etc. Therefore he [is] in mercy.

(c) *Vered<i>c<tu>m xij(mi) Qui quidem jur<atores> de div<er>sis artic<u>lis cur<iam> tangent<ibus> on<er>ati ven<iunt> et affirmant om<n>ia et sing<u>la p<er> officiarios p<re>d<i>c<t>os sup<er>ius p<re>sent<ata> fore vera et dic<unt> q<uo>d officiarii p<re>d<i>c<t>i bene et fidelit<er> p<re>sentav<er>unt et null<um> fec<er>unt concelament<um> ad notitiam jur<atorum> p<re>d<ictorum>*

Verdict of the 12. Which jurors, charged with the various articles touching the court, come and affirm all and singular presented by the aforesaid officers above to be true and they say that the aforesaid officers have well and faithfully presented and have concealed nothing to the knowledge of the aforesaid jurors.

(d) *Et ult<er>ius p<re>sent<ant> q<uo>d Edwardus Aston miles qui de d<omi>no tenuit p<er> copiam rot<u>li s<e>c<un>d<u>m cons<uetudinem> man<er>ij p<re>d<i>c<t>i un<um> messuagiu<m> ac prata eidem mes<suagio> spectant<ia> in Magna Heywood diem clausit extre<m>um citra ultim<am> cur<iam> post cui<us> mort accid<it> d<omi>no un<us> tauru<s> p<re>tij xxxiijs.ivd. no<m>i<n>e h<er>ietti*

And further they present that Edward Aston, knight, who held of the lord by copy of the roll according to the custom of the aforesaid manor a messuage and meadows belonging to the same messuage in Great Heywood has died since the last court, on whose death there falls due to the lord one bull worth 33s. 4d. in the name of heriot.

Exercise 11 (p. 15)

(a) *Ad hanc Cur<iam> ven<it> Joh<ann>es Welles, ar<miger>, p<er> Radulphum Right, Attornatum eius, et sursu<m> redd<idit> in manus d<omi>ni man<er>ij p<re>di<cti> unu<m> cottagiu<m> et unu<m> clausu<m> anglice a Croft ib<ide>m p<er>tinen<s> nup<er> in tenura Rob<er>ti Turner defunct<i>*

To this court came John Welles, esquire, by his attorney Ralph Right, and surrendered into the hands of the lord of the aforesaid manor one cottage and one close, in English a Croft, pertaining thereto, lately in the tenure of Robert Turner, deceased.

(b) *... unu<m> messuagiu<m> sive tenementu<m> cu<m> p<er>tin<entiis> iacen<s> et existen<s> in Morrey End infra man<er>iu<m> p<re>d<ictum> ad opus et usu<m> Will<elm>i Crooke et Cat<er>ine Crooke ux<oris> eius p<ro> et durant<e> termino vite naturalis eo<rum> et eo<rum> diutius viventiu<m>*

... one messuage or tenement with appurtenances lying and being in Morrey End within the manor aforesaid to the use and behoof of William Crooke and Catherine Crooke his wife, for and during the term of their natural lives and the life of the longer living of them ...

(c) *... unu<m> cottagiu<m> cu<m> p<er>tin<entiis> scituat<um> et existen<s> in ABCD p<re>d<icto> cu<m> o<mn>ib<us> domib<us> edificijs horreis stabul<is> gardin<ijs> pomar<ijs> cu<m> puteis corarijs anglice Tanfats ...*

... one cottage with appurtenances situated and being in ABCD aforesaid, with all houses, buildings, barns, stables, gardens, orchards, with leaching pits, in English tanning vats ...

(d) *... ac una<m> pastur<am> sive croftu<m> eid pertinen<tem> et adiacen<tem> ac unam peci<am> sive p<ar>cella<m> vasti adjacen<tem> eid cottagio ...*

... and one pasture or croft pertaining and next to the same and one piece or parcel of waste next to the same cottage ...

(e) *... ac unu<m> furnacia<m> vel humitoriu<m> (anglice one kiln house or Tanyard) ut nunc abbuttat anglice as it is now bounded et una<m> mandra<m> stant sup<er> sex postibus anglice a hovel standing upon six posts ...*

... and one kiln house or tanyard as it is now bounded and one hovel standing upon six posts ... (English not repeated)

Example 1 (p. 17)

(a) *Cur<ia> Visus Franc<i>pleg<ij> cu<m> Cur<ia> Baron<is> Oswaldi Mosley Bar<onetti> D<omi>ni Man<er>ij p<re>d<icti> tent<a> ib<ide>m p<ro> Man<er>io p<re>d<icto> Tricesimo die Octobris Anno regni D<omi>ni n<ost>ri Georgij S<e>c<un>di Dei Gratia Magn<e> Britanie Franc<ie> et Hib<er>nie Regis feidei defensor<is> etc. Quinto Annoq<ue> D<omi>ini 1731 Coram Ric<ard>o Nicholls Gen<eroso> S<enes>challo ib<ide>m*

Court of the view of frankpledge with court baron of Oswald Mosley, Baronet, lord of the aforesaid manor, held there for the aforesaid manor on the 30th day of October in the 5th year of the reign of our lord George II by the grace of God king of Great Britain, France, and Ireland, defender of the faith etc., and in the year of our lord 1731, before Richard Nicholls, gentleman, steward there.

(b)   *Magna cur<ia> de Burton' tent<a> die Sab<bat>i p<ro>x<ima> p<os>t f<estu>m s<an>c<t>i*
      M<ar>ci Ewang<eliste> anno r<egni> r<egis> E<dwardi> t<er>cij a conquestu t<er>tio et an<n>o
      W Abb<atis> xiij°

Great court of Burton held on Saturday next after the feast of Saint Mark the Evangelist in
the 3rd year of the reign of King Edward III after the Conquest [29 April 1329] and in the
13th year of Abbot W.

(c)   *Cur<ia> de Burton' tent<a> die Sab<bat>i p<ro>x<ima> p<os>t f<estu>m decollat<i>o<n>is*
      s<an>c<t>i Joh<annis> anno r<egni> r<egis> E<dwardi> t<er>cij a co<n>q<ue>stu t<er>cio

Court of Burton held on Saturday next after the feast of the beheading of Saint John in the
3rd year of the reign of King Edward III after the Conquest [2 September 1329].

(d)   *Cur<ia> de Burton' tent<a> die Sab<bat>i p<ro>x<ima> p<ost> f<es>t<u>m s<an>c<t>i*
      Augustini ep<iscop>i et co<n>fessor<is> anno sup<radi>cto

Court of Burton held on Saturday next after the feast of Saint Augustine, bishop and
confessor, in the above mentioned year [3 September 1328].

(e)   *Cur<ia> apud Alrewas die s<an>c<t>i Barnabe Ap<osto>li an<n>o Reg<ni> R<egis> H<enrici>*
      fil<ii> Reg<is> J<ohannis> xliij°

Court at Alrewas on the day of Saint Barnabas the Apostle in the 43rd year of the reign of
Henry son of King John [11 June 1259].

Example 2 (p. 19)
(a)   *Magna Cur<ia> de Burton' tent<a> die Sabb<at>i in f<est>o S<an>c<t>i Luce Ewangelist<e>*
      anno r<egni> E<dwardi> xx° et W. Abb<at>is xj
      Esson<ie>
      Henri<icus> de Norton se de co<mmun>i p<er> Ric<ardu>m
      Groucokes ij°
      Joh<ann>es at the Tounesende se de eod p<er> Joh<annem> le Broune j°
      Joh<ann>es de Wynsull se de eod p<er> Joh<ann>em de Hornyglowe ij°
      Henr<icus> fil<ius> Ric<ard>i se de eod p<er>
      Maur<icium> filiu<m> suu<m> j°
      Ric<ardus> Pilly<n>g def<icit> v<ersus> Abb<at>em de pla<c>ito t<ransgressio>nis p<er>
      Ad<am> ball<iv>iu<m>
      Rob<er>t<u>s le Listere se de co<mmun>i p<er> Ad<am> de molend<ino> capel<a>nu<m> ij°

Great court of Burton held on Saturday in the feast of Saint Luke the Evangelist in the 20th
year of the reign of Edward [18 October 1326] and the 11th of Abbot W[illiam].
Essoins. Henry of Norton [essoins] himself by Richard Groucokes 2nd [time].
John at the Townshend [essoins] himself of the same [suit of court] by John le Broune, 1st
[time].
John of Winshill [essoins] himself of the same [suit of court] by John of Horninglow 2nd
[time].
Henry son of Richard [essoins] himself of the same [suit of court] by Maurice his son 1st
[time].
Richard Pillyng defaults against the abbot in a plea of trespass by Adam the bailiff.
Robert the Lister [essoins] himself of common [suit of court] by Adam of the Mill, chaplain
2nd [time].

(b) *Visus frauncipleg<ii> cu<m> curia ib<ide>m tento die Jovis in septimana Pentecostis an<no> Regni Henrici octavi dei gra<tia> Angliae et Fraunciae ~~et Hiberniae~~ Reg<is> fidei defensor<is> d<omi>ni Hib<er>n<ie> et in terra sup<re>mi capit<is> eccl<es>iae Anglicane post conquestu<m> Anglie tricesimo tertio*

View of frankpledge with court held there on Thursday in Pentecost week in the 33rd year of the reign of Henry VIII [9 June 1541] by the grace of God of England and France, and Ireland *(crossed through)* king, defender of the faith and lord of Ireland, and on earth supreme head of the English church, after the conquest of England.

(c) *Visus f<ra>nci<pleggii> de Alrewas tent<us> die Lune in crastino s<an>c<t>i marie magdalene anno Reg<ni> R<egis> E<dwardi> t<er>tij post <con>q<uestum> quarto*
Esson<ie>. Walt<e>r<u>s Halpeny de app<arentia> Joh<anne>s Aldem de app<arentia> Henr<icus> Warde de app<arentia> Nich<olau>s de Tymmore Andreas Mogg Joh<anne>s le Cl<er>ic<us> Rob<ertu>s Falyn(?) Rob<ertu>s Warde de appar<entia> p<er> Ric<ard>u<m> Averel

View of frankpledge of Alrewas held on Monday on the morrow of Saint Mary Magdalen in the 4th year of the reign of king Edward III after the conquest [23 July 1330].
Essoins. Walter Halpeny for appearance; John Aldem for appearance; Henry Warde for appearance; Nicholas of Tymmore Andrew Mogg John the Clerk Robert Falyn (?) Robert Warde for appearance by Richard Averill.

(d) *Rob<ertus> pistor ess<oniat> se p<er> Ric<ardu>m cl<er>icu<m> de secta cur<ie> p<ri>mo*
Ada<m> fil<ius> Reginald<i> ess<oniat> se p<er> Will<elmu>m
fil<ium> Nich<olai> bigarii de eod p<ri>mo
Will<elmus> Edrian ess<oniat> se de communi secta p<er>
Adekein fil<ium> suu<m> j°
Will<elmus> Ada<m> ess<oniat> se p<er> Hugone<m> messore<m> de eod j°
Rob<ertus> fil<ius> Reginald<i> ess<oniat> se de eod p<er> Will<elmu>m fil<ium> Rob<er>ti fil<ii> Rad<ulph>i p<ri>mo
Will<elmus> Fox ess<oniat> se p<er> Will<elmu>m Owen v<ersu>s M<ar>g<er>iam sorore<m> sua<m> de placito t<er>re p<ri>mo

Robert [the] baker essoins himself by Richard [the] clerk of suit of court first [time].
Adam son of Reginald essoins himself by William son of Nicholas the carter of the same, first [time].
William Edrian essoins himself of common suit [of court] by Adekein his son, 1st [time].
William Adam essoins himself by Hugh the hayward of the same 1st [time].
Adam son of Reginald essoins himself of the same by William son of Robert son of Radulph, first [time].
William Fox essoins himself by William Owen against Margery his sister in a plea of land, first [time].

Example 3 (p. 21)
(a) *Thom<as> atthewalle el<ec>t<u>s est p<re>p<ositu>s de Horny<n>glowe et Wehtm<er>e vid<e>l<ice>t de redd<itibus> co<n>suetudi<n>ib<us> finib<us> et p<er>q<ui>sitis cur<ie>*

Thomas Atthewalle was elected reeve of Horninglow and Wetmore namely for the rents customs fines and profits of the court.

(b) *Rob<er>t<u>s s<upe>r le grene el<ec>t<u>s est g<ra>ngiar<ius> de Schob<nall> et Jur<atus>*
    Ad<a>m Hobbesson el<ec>t<u>s est g<ra>ngiar<ius> de Stretton

Robert on the Green was elected granger of Shobnall and sworn; Adam Hobbesson was
elected granger of Stretton.

Example 4 (p. 21)

(a) *Franciscus Bartelett cunstabul<arius> ib<ide>m Jur<atus> present<at> sup<er> sacr<amentum>*
    suu<m> q<uo>d omnia b<e>ne

Francis Bartelett constable there, sworn, presents on his oath that all [is] well.

(b) *Rog<er>us Umfrey p<ro> t<ra>ns<gressione> p<er> aucas suas in blado et p<ra>to d<omi>ni*
    i<de>o in mi<sericordi>a
    Will<elmu>s Snow p<ro> t<ra>ns<gressione> p<er> aucas i<n> blado et prato d<omi>ni i<de>o in
    mi<sericordi>a
    Marg<ar>ta del halle p<ro> t<ra>ns<gressione> p<er> aucas suas ibid<e>m i<de>o in
    mi<sericordi>a
    Rob<ertu>s Enge p<ro> t<ra>ns<gressione> p<er> aucas suas ibid<e>m i<de>o in mi<sericordi>a
    Joh<anne>s cementar<ius> p<ro> t<ra>ns<gressione> p<er> aucas suas ibidem i<de>o in
    mi<sericordi>a
    Will<elmu>s Pollard p<ro> t<ra>ns<gressione> p<er> aucas suas ibid in mi<sericordi>a
    Joh<anne>s le Parson p<ro> t<ra>ns<gressione> p<er> ~~aucas suas~~ *ij vitulos/ ibid in*
    mi<sericordi>a

Roger Umfrey for trespass by his geese in the cornfield and meadow of the lord therefore
[he is] in mercy.
William Snow for trespass by [his] geese in the cornfield and meadow of the lord therefore
[he is] in mercy.
Margaret del Halle for trespass by her geese there, therefore [she is] in mercy.
Robert Enge for trespass by his geese there, therefore [he is] in mercy.
John the mason for trespass by his geese there, therefore [he is] in mercy.
William Pollard for trespass by his geese there [therefore he is] in mercy.
John the parson for trespass by his geese *(crossed through)* two calves there, in mercy.

(c) *It<e>m p>sent<at> Ric<ard>u<m> Austin p<ro> def<ec>tu in fensura eius inter Bond feild et*
    Bridgefeild iuxta pena<m> nostra<m>

Likewise he presents Richard Austin for a gap in his fence between Bond field and
Bridgefield according to our penalty.

(d) *Jur<atores> p<redicti> sup<er> sac<ramenta> sua p<re>sent<ant> quod Joh<ann>es Allman*
    fil<ius> Ric<ard>i Allman defunct<i> et un<us> customar<ius> tenens Maner<ii> p<re>d<icti>
    obijt citra ult<imam> Curia<m> et quod sup<er> obitum p<re>d<icti> Joh<ann>is accidit
    dom<ino> Man<er>ij p<re>d<icti> optimu<m> animal sive optimu<m> ejus bovum p<ro>
    Herriett<o>

The aforesaid jurors on their oaths present that John Allman son of Richard Allman
deceased and a customary tenant of the aforesaid manor died since the last court and that on
the death of the aforesaid John there falls to the lord of the aforesaid manor the best animal
or his best ox for a heriot.

Example 5 (p. 23)

(a) *Ad hanc Cur<iam> ven<it> Will<elm>us Normansell de Wolv<er>hampton in Com<itatu> p<re>d<icto> Mercer in p<ro>pria p<er>sona sua et sursu<m> Redd<idit> in manus d<omi>ne man<er>ij p<re>d<icti> quatuor Acras terre iacen<tes> in quodam Clauso vocat<o> le Leyes Dispersim nup<er> in tenura sive occupac<i>one Thome Ruynton ad opus et usu<m> p<re>fat<i> Thome Ruynton*

To this court came William Normansell of Wolverhampton in the aforesaid county and surrendered into the hands of the lady of the aforesaid manor four acres of land lying here and there in a certain close called Le Leyes lately in the tenure or occupation of Thomas Ruynton to the use and behoof of the said Thomas Ruynton.

(b) *Ad hanc Cur<iam> ven<it> Samuel<us> Lathropp de Leigh in Com<itatu> Staff<ordie> gen<erosus> et cepit de d<omi>no man<er>ij p<re>d<icti> medietat duo<rum> messuagio<rum> sive Ten<emen>to<rum> cu<m> p<er>tinen<cijs> vocat<orum> halswayne things iacen<tium> in Reeve End infra man<er>iu<m> de Yoxall p<re>d<icto> ac medietate<m> unius Cottagij cu<m> medietat o<m>niu<m> domo<rum> edificio<rum> gardin<orum> horreo<rum> pomar<iorum> croft<orum> terr<arum> ten<emen>to<rum> prat<orum> pascu<arum> et pastur<arum> cu<m> p<er>tinen<cijs> eis<dem> spectan<tibus> sive aliquo modo p<er>tinen<tibus> in Yoxall p<re>d<icto>*

To this court came Samuel Lathropp of Leigh in the county of Stafford, gentleman, and received from the lord of the aforesaid manor a moiety of two messuages or tenements with appurtenances called halswayn things in Reeve End within the manor or Yoxall aforesaid and a moiety of one cottage with a moiety of all houses, buildings, gardens, barns, orchards, crofts, lands, tenements, meadows, grazing lands and pastures, with appurtenances belonging or in any way pertaining to the same in Yoxall aforesaid.

(c) *... H<ab>end<um> et tenend<um> p<re>d<ictam> medietat duo<rum> messuag<iorum> sive Ten<emen>to<rum> p<re>d<ictorum> cu<m> medietat<e> Cottagij p<re>d<icti> ac medietat<e> o<m>niu<m> et sing<u>lo<rum> p<re>misso<rum> p<re>d<ictorum> cu<m> p<er>tinen<cijs> p<re>fato Samuel<o> Lathropp hered<ibus> et assign<atis> suis imp<er>petuu<m> ad voluntate<m> d<omi>ni s<e>c<un>d<u>m cons<uetudinem> man<er>ij p<re>d<icti> p<er> Reddit<us> rep<ar>ac<i>ones et o<mn>ia al<ia> servicia inde prius debit<a> et de iure consuet<a>. Et ad decessu<m> ip<s>ius Samuel<i> duo ex optimis suis animalib<us> sive bovis p<ro> herriott<o> p<ro> utroq<ue> messuag<io> sive Ten<emen>t<o> cu<m> p<er>tinen<cijs> vel quinq<ue> libras ad elecc<i>o<n>e<m> d<omi>ni man<er>ij p<re>d<icti> Et dedit d<omi>no de fine ad ingr<essu>m* (blank) *Et admissus est inde Tenens fecitq<ue> d<omi>no fidelitate<m>*

To have and to hold the aforesaid moiety of the two aforesaid messuages or tenements with a moiety of the aforesaid cottage and a moiety of all and singular the aforesaid premises with appurtenances, to the aforesaid Samuel Lathropp, his heirs and assigns in perpetuity, at the will of the lord, according to the custom of the aforesaid manor, by the rents, repairs and all services thence formerly owed and by right accustomed. And at the death of the same Samuel two of his best beasts or oxen for a heriot for each messuage or tenement with appurtenances or £5 at the choice of the lord of the aforesaid manor. And he gave to the lord at his entry (blank) and was admitted thence tenant and did fealty.

Example 6 (p. 25)

Ad hanc Cur<iam> venit Joh<ann>es Plummer in p<ro>p<r>ia p<er>sona sua in plen<a> Cur<ia>
sursum reddidit in manus D<omi>ni Man<er>ij p<re>dict<i> p<er> virgam s<e>c<un>d<u>m
consuetud<inem> Man<er>ij p<re>dict<i> un<am> Dolam prati cu<m> p<er>tin<entiis> in Burway
Meadow jacen<tem> sup<er> Longmoore ... ib<ide>m et un<am> al<iam> Dolam prati in eod<e>m
prato jacen<tem> sup<er> le Smeeth ib<ide>m int<er> terr<am> olim Will<elm>i Daniell ex una p<ar>te
et terr<am> D<omi>ni Man<er>ij pr<e>d<icti> ex alt<era> p<ar>te un<am> al<iam> Dolam prati
jacen<tem> in prato vocat<o> Longlake Int<er> terr<am> ib<ide>m olim Hen<ri>ci Smith ex una
p<ar>te et Terr<am> Joh<ann>is Mousley ex alt<era> p<ar>te et un<am> al<iam> Dol<am> prati in
eodem prato jacen<tem> int<er> terr<am> olim p<re>d<icti> Hen<ri>ci Smith ex una p<ar>te et
terr<am> hered<um> Thome Bayley Defunct<i> ex alter<a> p<ar>te cum p<er>tin<entiis> ad opus et
usum Joh<ann>is Shemonds Hered<um> et assignato<rum> suor<um> In p<er>petuu<m> Et sup<er>
hoc in ista ead<e>m Curia ven<it> p<re>d<ictus> Joh<ann>es Shemonds in p<ro>p<r>ia p<er>sona sua
et in plen<a> Cur<ia> petit admitti tenen<s> p<re>missis p<re>d<ictis> cu<m> p<er>tin<entiis> Cui
D<omi>nus Man<er>ij p<re>d<icti> p<er> S<enes>callum suum p<re>d<ictum> concessit inde
sei<sin>am p<er> virgam s<e>c<un>d<u>m consuetudin Man<er>ij p<re>d<icti>
H<ab>end<um> et tenend<um> p<re>missa p<re>d<icta> cu<m> p<er>tin<entiis> p<re>fat<o>
Joh<ann>i Shemonds Hered<ibus> et assignat<is> suis Imp<er>petuu<m> ad voluntat D<omi>ni
s<e>c<un>d<u>m consuet<udinem> Man<er>ij p<re>d<ic>ti et p<ro> redditu Herriot<to> et al<ia>
servic<ia> inde prius debit<a> et de jure consuet<a> et dat D<omi>no p<ro> fine ad Ingress<um>
(blank) Et post tres p<ro>clamac<i>ones inde prius fact<as> s<e>c<un>d<u>m consuet<udinem>
Man<er>ij p<re>d<icti> admiss<us> est inde tenens et fec<it> D<omi>no fidelitat etc.

To this court came John Plummer in his own person [and] in open court surrendered into
the hands of the lord of the manor aforesaid by the rod according to the custom of the
aforesaid manor one dole of meadow with appurtenances in Burway Meadow lying upon
Longmoore ... there and one other dole of meadow in the same meadow lying upon the
Smeeth there between the land formerly belonging to William Daniell on the one side and
the land of the lord of the aforesaid manor on the other side, one other dole of meadow
lying in the meadow called Longlake between the land there formerly belonging to Henry
Smith on the one side and the land of John Mousley on the other side and one other dole of
meadow in the same meadow lying between the land formerly belonging to the aforesaid
Henry Smith on the one side and the land of the heirs of Thomas Bayley deceased on the
other side with appurtenances to the use and behoof of John Shemonds his heirs and assigns
forever. And on this the aforesaid John Shemonds came into the court in his own person and
in open court asked to be admitted tenant to the aforesaid premises with appurtenances to
whom the lord of the aforesaid manor, by his aforesaid steward, granted thence seisin by the
rod according to the custom of the manor aforesaid to have and to hold the aforesaid
premises with appurtenances to the aforesaid John Shemonds and his heirs and assigns
forever, at the will of the lord according to the custom of the aforesaid manor and for the
rent, heriot and other service formerly owed and by right accustomed, and he gives to the
lord for a fine at his entry (blank). And after three proclamations thence first made
according to the custom of the aforesaid manor he was admitted thence tenant and did
fealty to the lord etc.

Example 7 (p. 27)

Nich<ola>us Bold et Rob<er>tus Byddell decennar<ii> ib<ide>m jur<ati> p<re>sent<ant> Thomam (jd.) Clerke Henr<icum> Chatcall p<ro> def<ec>tu apparant<ie> i<de>o ip<s>i in m<isericord>ia d<omi>ni It<e>m p<re>sent<ant> q<uo>d Joh<ann>es (viijd.) Browne tenet co<mmun>e<m> hospitiu<m> et vend<it> victual<ia> ad p<re>tiu<m> excessivu<m> I<de>o ip<s>e in m<isericord>ia d<omi>ni It<e>m p<re>sent<ant> Ed<wa>r<d>us (iiijd.) Hill Franciscus (iiijd.) Bright et Elizabeth<a> (iiijd.) Assheton vid<ua> sunt co<mmun>es bras<iatores> s<er>visie et freg<er>unt assi<s>am I<de>o quilib<e>t eo<rum> in m<sericord>ia d<omi>ni It<e>m p<re>sent<ant> Jervasiu<m> (iiijd.) Olyver p<ro> vend<itione> carnis ad p<re>tiu<m> excessivu<m> I<de>o ip<s>e in mi<sericord>ia d<omi>ni

Nicholas Bold and Robert Byddell tithingmen there [having been] sworn present Thomas Clerke, Henry Chatcull for default of appearance therefore they [are] in mercy of the lord. Likewise they present that John (8d.) Browne keeps a common lodging house and sells victuals at excessive price therefore he [is] in mercy of the lord. Likewise they present [that] Edward (4d.) Hill, Francis (4d.) Bright and Elizabeth (4d.) Assheton widow are common brewers of ale and broke the assize therefore each of them [is] in mercy of the lord. Likewise they present Jervase (4d.) Olyver for selling meat at excessive price. Therefore he [is] in mercy of the lord.

Example 8 (p. 27)

Et q<uo>d Ric<ard>us (ijd.) Messing obstupavit via<m> ecclesiastica<m> ducent a ten<emen>to voc<ato> Corbettes usq<ue> eccl<es>iam de Boxted I<de>o in m<isericord>ia d<omi>ni p<ro>ut in capite.
Et p<receptum> est ball<iv>io p<re>monere p<re>d<i>c<tu>m Ric<ardu>m Messing ad ap<er>iend<um> et deponend<um> via<m> p<re>d<i>c<t>am p<ro>ut fuit ab antiquo temp<or>e citra festu<m> s<anc>te trinitat<is> p<ro>x<imum> futur<um> sub pena forisf<acture> d<omi>no iijs.iiijd.
Et p<receptum> est ball<iv>io p<re>monere p<re>d<i>c<tu>m Ric<ard>u<m> Messing ad ligand<um> cane<m> suu<m> nec q<uo>d de cetero no<n> mordet nec ledit aliq<uem> legio<rum> d<omi>no Regis sub pena fo<risfactur<arum> d<omi>no iijs.iiijd.

And that Richard (2d.) Messing obstructed the church road leading from the tenement called Corbettes to the church of Boxsted. Therefore [he is] in mercy as [appears] above [his name].
And the bailiff is ordered to warn the aforesaid Richard Messing to open and restore the aforesaid road as it was from ancient time, before the feast of the Holy Trinity next to come under penalty of a fine of 3s. 4d. to the lord.
And the bailiff is ordered to warn the aforesaid Richard Messing to tie up his dog so that in future it shall not bite nor injure any of the lord king's liegemen under penalty of fines of 3s. 4d. to the lord.

Example 9 (p. 29)

Prima curia Thome Lovell armig<er>i filij et hered<is> Francisci Lovell cu<m> attornament<o> tenent<ium> ib<ide>m tent<a> die Jovis in Septima<na> pasche anno Regni Edwardi Sexti dei gra<tia> Anglie Francie et hib<er>nie Regis fidei defens<oris> et in terra Eccl<es>ie Anglicane et hibernice sup<re>mi capit<is> post conqu<estum> Sexto Antonius Remyngton, iur<e> ux<or>is, esson<iatus> p<er> R<o>b<er>tu<m> Sowgate
Attornament<a> tenent<ium>
Ad hanc curiam om<n>es tam libe<ri> q<ua>m nat<ivi> ten<entes> et firmar<ii> exact<i> fuerunt, de

quib<us> comp<ar>uer<unt> Rob<ert>us Fynche et Thomas Proude firmarij Scitus man<er>ij et
terr<arum> d<o>m<in>ical<ium>, Will<elm>us Johnson Rob<er>tus Sowgate Joh<ann>es Jackson
Cl<er>icu<s>. Will<elm>us (lib<er>) Pyrrynt Rob<er>tus (li<ber>) Brome Thomas [lib<er>] Sherff (?)
Joh<ann>es (lib<er>) Burton Ed<ward>us Page Andreas Grey, Will<elm>us Redma<n>, dur<ante>
minor<e> etate Anne Spycer, Thomas Wryght, et Will<elm>us Wryght et se attornaverunt tenentes
p<re>fati Thome Lovell

First court of Thomas Lovell Esquire son and heir of Francis Lovell with tenant attornment
there held on Thursday in Easter week in the sixth year of the reign of Edward VI by the
grace of God of England, France and Ireland, king, defender of the faith and on earth
supreme head of the English and Irish church after the conquest [21 April 1552]. Antony
Remyngton in right of his wife was essoined by Robert Sowgate.
Tenant acknowledgements were demanded at this court [of] all tenants both free and villein
and [of] farmers of whom appeared Robert Fynche and Thomas Proude, farmers of the site
of the manor and the demesne lands, William Johnson, Robert Sowgate, John Jackson, clerk,
William Pyrrynt, [freeholder], Robert Brome [freeholder], Thomas Sherff (?) [freeholder],
John Burton [freeholder], Edward Page, Andrew Grey, William Redman, during [their]
minority, Anne Spycer, Thomas Wryght, and William Wryght, [and] acknowledged
[themselves to be] tenants of the aforesaid Thomas Lovell.

Example 10 (p. 31)
Franciplegii d<e> Alrewas p<resentant> q<uo>d Isabell<a> (xijd.) que fuit ux<or> Thom<e> de
Ridewar<e> que debet app<arentiam> no<n> ve<nit> id<e>o in m<isericord>ia It<e>m p<resentant>
q<uo>d Joh<anne>s Hugonis (vjd.) non ve<nit> id<e>o in m<isericord>ia. It<e>m p<resentant>
q<uo>d Henr<icus> le pyncker<narius> (xijd.) t<ra>xit sang<uinem> iniust<e> de Will<elm>o Paty
id<e>o in m<isericord>ia p<er> pl<egios> Galfr<idi> de S<tre>tton (?) et Thom<e> Gyn It<e>m
p<resentant> q<uo>d Agnes fil<ia> Ric<ard>i Hub<er>t le<vavit> hu<tesium> iust<e> s<upe>r
Alic<iam> Cullecart (iiijd.) q<uia> paup<er> id<e>o in m<isercord>ia p<er> pl<egios> Gilb<ert>i
s<upe>r le hethy et Galf<ridi> Goderone It<e>m p<resentant> q<uo>d d<ic>ta Alic<ia> le<vavit>
hu<tesium> iust<e> s<upe>r Joh<anne>m Hubert (vjd.) et Agn<etam> (vjd.) sorore<m> ei<us> id<e>o
eo q<uo>d ijd<e>m Joh<anne>s et Agnes fec<er>unt s<upe>r ip<s>am hamsocna<m> id<e>o ambo in
m<isericord>ia p<er> pl<egios> Ric<ard>i Hub<er>t et Ric<ardi> le prest. It<e>m p<resentant> q<uo>d
Henr<icus> le Rop<er>e le<vavit> hu<tesium> i<us>te s<upe>r Will<elmu>m Paty (vjd.) id<e>o
d<i>c<t>us Will<elmu>s in m<isericord>ia p<er> pl<egios> Galfr<idi> de S<tre>tton et Thom<e> Colyn.
It<e>m p<resentant> q<uo>d Joh<anne>s de C<o>ton (vjd.) t<ra>xit sang<uinem> iniust<e> de
Ric<ardo> Averel id<e>o d<i>c<t>us Joh<anne>s in m<isericord>ia p<er> pl<egios> Thom<e> le clerc et
Ric<ardi> Av<er>il. It<e>m p<resentant> q<uo>d Will<elmu>s (xijd.) fil<ius> Will<elmi> Goderone
t<ra>xit sang<uinem> iniust<e> de Ric<ard>o Hubert id<e>o d<i>c<t>us Will<elmu>s in
m<isericord>ia p<er> pl<egios> p<at>r<i>s sui et Galfr<idi> fr<atr>is sui. It<e>m p<resentant> q<uo>d
Matild<a> le Rop<er>e le<vavit> hu<tesium> i<us>te s<upe>r Marg<eriam> (vjd.) ux<or>e<m>
Ric<ard>i Averel id<e>o d<ic>ta Marg<eria> in m<isericord>ia p<er> pl<egios> Thom<e> Clerc et
Ric<ardi> Av<er>il It<e>m p<resentant> q<uo>d d<ic>ta Matild<a> t<ra>xit sang<uinem> (vjd.)
q<uia> paup<er> iniust<e> de d<i>cta Marg<eria> id<e>o d<ic>ta Matild<a> in m<isericord>ia p<er>
pl<egios> Thom<e> le clerc et Henr<ici> Bernard. It<e>m p<resentant> q<uo>d Will<elmu>s Abbot
(vjd.) le<vavit> hu<tesium> iniust<e> s<upe>r Ric<ardum> Arkell Joh<anne>m Deyis (?) et
Ric<ardum> Sparke et alios ign<otos> id<e>o d<i>c<t>us Will<elmu>s in m<isericord>ia p<er>
pl<egios> Thom<e> Colyn et Thom<e> Gyn sen<ioris>. It<e>m p<resentant> q<uo>d d<i>c<t>us
Will<elmu>s Abbot (xijd.) venit a Croxh<all> a concubina sua uxore<m> sua<m> Agnet<am> obivavit
ap<u>d Saltbrugg<e> et ip<s>am vi et violentia p<er>cussit et ex ea iniust<e> sang<uninem> t<ra>xit
et ip<s>am ibi occidere et necar<e> voluit. Id<e>o d<i>c<t>us Will<elmu>s in m<isericord>ia p<er>
pl<egios> Ric<ardi> F<ra>ncis et Ade ...

The tithingmen of Alrewas present that Isabel (12d.) who was the wife of Thomas de Rideware who owes appearance has not come therefore [she is] in mercy. Likewise they present that John Hugh (6d.) has not come therefore [he is] in mercy. Likewise they present that Henry the butler (12d.) unjustly drew blood from William Paty therefore [he is] in mercy by the pledges of Geoffrey de Stretton [and] Thomas Gyn. Likewise they present that Agnes daughter of Richard Hubert justly raised the hue and cry against Alice Cullecart (4d.) because [she is a] pauper therefore [she is] in mercy by the pledges' of Gilbert on the Heath and Geoffrey Goderone. Likewise they present that the said Alice justly raised the hue and cry against John Hubert (6d.) and Agnes (6d.) his sister, therefore because the same John and Agnes broke into [her] house both [are] in mercy by the pledges of Richard Hubert andRichard the priest. Likewise they present that Henry the roper justly raised the hue and cry against William Paty (6d.) therefore the said William [is] in mercy by the pledges of Geoffrey of Stretton and Thomas Colyn. Likewise they present that John of C[ot]ton (6d.) unjustly drew blood from Richard Averel therefore the said John [is] in mercy by the pledges of Thomas the clerk and Richard Averil. Likewise they present that William (12d.) son of William Goderone unjustly drew blood from Richard Hubert therefore the said William [is] in mercy by the pledges of his father and Geoffrey his brother. Likewise they present that Matilda le roper justly raised the hue and cry against Margery (6d.) wife of Richard Averel therefore the said Margery [is] in mercy by the pledges·of Thomas clerk and Richard Averil. Likewise they present that the said Matilda ((6d.) because [she is a] pauper) unjustly drew blood from the said Margery therefore the said Matilda [is] in mercy by the pledges of Thomas the clerk and Henry Bernard. Likewise they present that William Abbot (6d.) unjustly raised the hue and cry against Richard Arkell John Deyis and Richard Spark and other unknown persons therefore the said William [is] in mercy by the pledges of Thomas Colyn and Thomas Gyn senior. Likewise they present that the said William Abbot (12d.) came from Croxhall from his concubine, met his wife Agnes at Saltbridge, and struck her with force and violence and unjustly drew blood from her and wanted to kill and murder her. Therefore the said William [is] in mercy by the pledges of Richard Francis and Adam ...

Example 11 (p. 33)
Burton' Curi<ia> magna<a> tent<a> ib<ide>m inf<ra> Abbath<iam> die Sab<ba>ti in festo S<anc>ti Luce Ewang<e>l<ist>e a<nn>o r<egni> r<egis> Ric<ard>i s<e>c<un>di post conq<uestum> xvij Et Thom<e> de South<a>m abb<at>is xxviij°

Esson<ie> John<anne>s Pyp<er> de Annesley de co<mmun>i p<er> clericu<m> Thom<a>s Ryder de co<mmun>i p<er> clericu<m> Rob<er>tus Penyfot de eod p<er> clericu<m> Joh<anne>s de Botteslowe de co<mmun>i p<er> clericu<m> Rog<er>us de Creyghton de eod p<er> clericu<m> m<isericordia>ijd.

Joh<anne>s de Rubbeley de Wynshull q<ueritur> de Thom<a> (ijd.) de Curburgh de Stap<enhill> in pl<acit>o deb<it>i Qui sum<monitus> no<n> ven<it> i<de>o in m<isericord>ia Et p<receptum> ip<s>u<m> dis<tringere> cont<ra> p<ro>x<imam>

Inquis<itio>

Nich<ola>us Thaccher de Wyghtmer q<ueritur> de Ric<ard>o de Sparh<a>m de ead in pl<acit>o t<ra>ns<gressionis> Et dic<it> q<uo>d ip<s>e et manupasti sui eid detenuer<unt> una<m> mariol p<er> iij a<nn>os elaps<os> ad damp<na> sua xs. Qui dic<it> q<uo>d no<n> cul<pabilis> un<de> inquis<itio>

m<isericordia> ijd.

Joh<anne>s Hannesone de Annesley q<ueritur> de Joh<anne> Wryght (ijd.) de ead in pl<acit>o deb<it>i qui sum<monitus> est et no<n> ven<it> i<de>o in m<isericord>ia et p<receptum> ip<su>m dis<tringere> cont<ra> p<ro>x<imam> postea ven<it> et cogn<ovit> debitu<m> i<de>o in m<isericord>ia

m<isericordia> ijd.

Joh<anne>s (ijd.) Wryght de Annesley q<ueritur> de Joh<ann>e Hannesone de ead in pl<acit>o
t<ra>ns<gressionis> Qui quid Joh<anne>s Wryght in m<isericord>ia q<uia> no<n>
p<ro>s<ecutus> v<er>sus Joh<anne>m Hannesone p<re>d<ic>t<u>m
Inquis<itio>
Joh<anne>s atte Milne de Stretton q<ueritur> de Will<elm>o Sharle de ead in pl<acit>o
t<ra>ns<gressionis> Et dic<it> q<uo>d int<er>fecit unu<m> pullu<m> suu<m> cu<m> uno bov<e> suo
ad dampn<um> viijs. qui dic<it> q<uo>d no<n> cul<pabilis> un(de) inquis<itio>

Burton. Great court held there within the abbey on Saturday in the feast of St Luke the
Evangelist in the 17th year of the reign of King Richard II after the Conquest and the 28th of
Abbot Thomas of Southam [18 October 1393]. Essoins. John Pyp[er] of Annesley of
common [suit of court] by the clerk. Thomas Olyver of common [suit of court] by the clerk
(crossed through). Robert Penyfot of the same by the clerk. John of Botteslowe of common
[suit of court] by the clerk. Roger of Creyghton of the same by the clerk.
Mercy 2d. John of Rubbeley of Winshill complains of Thomas (2d.) of Curborough of
Stap[enhill] in a plea of debt, who was summoned and has not come therefore [he is] in
mercy and it is ordered to distrain him before the next [court].
Inquiry. Nicholas Thaccher of Wetmore complains of Richard of Sparham of the same
[place] in a plea of trespass and says that he and his household have detained from him one
unmated goose for three years past to his damage of 10s., who says that he is not guilty
therefore [there is to be an] inquiry.
Mercy 2d. John Hanneson of Annesley complains of John Wryght (2d.) of the same [place]
in a plea of debt, who was summoned and has not come therefore [he is] in mercy.
Afterwards he came and acknowledged the debt.
Mercy 2d. John (2d.) Wryght of Annesley complains of John Hannesone of the same [place]
in a plea of trespass, which John Wryght [is] in mercy because he has not prosecuted [his
action] against the aforesaid John Hannesone.
Inquiry. John at the Mill of Stretton complains of William Sharle of the same [place] in a
plea of trespass and says that he killed his foal with his ox to his damage 8s. who says that he
is not guilty and therefore [there is to be an] inquiry.

Example 12 (p. 35)
Visus franc<i>pleg<ij> cu<m> Cur<ia> Baron<is> Rad<ulph>i Sneyde Ar<migeri> d<omi>ni
maner<ij> p<re>d<i>c<t>i tent<us> ib<ide>m vicesimo septimo die Aprilis Anno R<eg>ni d<omi>ni
n<ost>ri Caroli dei grat<ia> Angl<ie> Scotie Franc<ie> et Hib<er>nie Reg<is> fidei defensor<is> etc.
duodecimo Coram Joh<ann>e Bell gen<eroso>

Will<elm>us Swyn<er>ton	
Thomas Rowley	*Jur<ati>i*
Thomas Smyth	
Randulph Burslem	
Will<elm>us Sault	
Thomas Boulton	*Jur<ati>i*
Joh<ann>es Stubbs	
Joh<ann>es Foard	
Joh<ann>es Hardinge	
Ed<wa>r<d>us Sympson	*Jur<ati>i*
Thomas Peake	
Rad<ulph>us Reeve	
Thomas Reeve	

Impr<im>is Jur<atores> dicunt et sup<er> sacr<ament>u<m> suu<m> putant q<uo>d Joh<ann>es Offley Mil<es> Will<elm>us Bowyer Miles hered<es> de Knutton Tenentes de Onneley Ed<wa>r<d>us Brett Ar<miger> Rad<ulph>us Smith gen<erosus> Reginald Mostons Thomas Hemings sunt Customar<ij> ten<en>tes huius Manerij et debent sectam huic Cur<ie> Et Ad hanc Cur<iam> non comp<aru>er<unt> sed default<am> fec<er>unt I<de>o ip<s>i et eoru<m> quilib<e>t sunt in m<isericord>ia d<omi>ni p<ro>ut patet sup<er> eor<um> capitib<us>

Ite<m> putant q<uo>d Ed<wa>r<d>us Cowp<er> Joh<ann>es Hewett Joh<ann>es Cowp<er> Ed<wa>r<d>us Foarde Thomas Heminges vendider<unt> panem et Cervic<iam> et freger<unt> assis<as> Ite<m> putant q<uo>d Ric<ard>us Hassall fecit affraiam sup<er> Lawrenc<ium> Rowley I<de>o etc.

Ite<m> putant q<uo>d Lawrenc<ius> Rowley fecit affraiam sup<er> Ric<ard>u<m> Hassall I<de>o etc. Ite<m> putant q<uo>d Joh<ann>es Wright fecit affraiam sup<er> Ed<wa>r<d>um Heath et traxit sanguinem I<de>o etc.

Ite<m> putant q<uo>d ad hanc Cur<iam> venit Rob<er>tus Morgan de Keele unus Customar<ius> ten<en>t<iar>iu<s> huius maner<ij> et s<e>c<un>d<u>m consuetud<inem> eiusdem maner<ij> sursu<m> reddidit in manus d<omi>ni p<re>d<i>c<t>i manerij totu<m> illud customar<ium> messuag<ium> cu<m> p<er>tin<entiis> iacen<s> et existen<s> in Keele

View of frankpledge with court baron of Ralph Sneyde Esquire, lord of the aforesaid manor, held there on the 27th day of April in the 12th year of the reign of our lord Charles [1636] by the grace of God king of England, Scotland, France and Ireland, defender of the faith etc. before John Bell, gentleman.

William Swynerton	
Thomas Rowley	sworn
Thomas Smyth	
Randulph Burslem	
William Sault	
Thomas Boulton	sworn
John Stubbs	
John Foard	
John Hardinge	
Edward Sympson	sworn
Thomas Peake	
Ralph Reeve	
Thomas Reeve	

First the jurors say and on their oath believe that John Offley, knight, William Bowyer, knight, the heirs of Knutton, the tenants of Onneley, Edward Brett, Esquire, Ralph Smith, gentleman, Reginald Mostons, Thomas Hemings are customary tenants of this manor and owe suit to this court and have not appeared at this court but have made default therefore they and each of them are in mercy of the lord as appears above [their names].

Likewise they believe that Edward Cowper, John Hewett, John Cowper Edward Foarde, Thomas Hemminges sold bread and ale and broke the assizes.

Likewise they believe that Richard Hassall assaulted Lawrence Rowley therefore etc.

Likewise they believe that Lawrence Rowley assaulted Richard Hassall therefore etc.

Likewise they believe that John Wright assaulted Edward Heath and drew blood therefore etc.

Likewise they believe that to this court came Robert Morgan of Keele a customary tenant of this manor and according to the custom of the same manor surrendered into the hands of the aforesaid lord of the manor all that customary messuage with appurtenances lying and being in Keele.

Example 13 (p. 37)

Maner<ium> de Tutbury cur<ia> Parva D<omi>ni Regis Angli<e> tent<a> apud Tutbury p<ro>
man<er>io p<re>d<icto> decimo nono die Januarij anno regni d<omi>ni n<ost>ri Jacobi s<e>c<un>d<i>
nunc Regis Angli<e> etc. secundo coram Ed<wa>r<d>o Foden cl<er>ic<o> ib<ide>m in p<re>sent<ia>
Hen<ri>ci Harlowe et Georgij Harlowe customar<iorum> tenen<tium> man<er>ij p<re>d<icti>

Ad hanc cur<iam> vener<unt> Samuel Emery pater et Samuel Emery filius ip<s>ius Samueli patris in
p<ro>pr<iis> p<er>son<is> suis et sursu<m> reddid<e>r<unt> in manus d<omi>ni maner<ij>
p<re>d<icti> p<er> virgam s<e>c<un>d<u>m consuetud<inem> maner<ij> p<re>d<icti> unu<m>
mes<suagium> sive ten<emen>tu<m> cu<m> p<er>tin<entiis> et duas p<ar>cell<as> t<er>re juxt<a>
Belmote lane co<mmun>it<er> voc<atum> Poole Milne Crofte et Tippers Riddings infr<a> man<eriu>m
de Tutbury p<re>d<icto> cu<m> o<mn>ib<us> et sing<u>lis suis p<er>tin<entiis> ad opus et usu<m>
Ric<ard>i Wakefeild gen<erosi> hered<um> et assign<atorum> suo<rum> imp<er>petuu<m> ad
volunt<atem> d<omi>ni s<e>c<un>d<u>m cons<uetudinem> man<er>ij p<re>d<icti> et sic remanet in
manib<us> D<omi>ni man<er>ij p<re>d<icti> et sup<er> hoc (in) ista<m> et ea<n>d<e>m cur<iam>
venit p<re>d<ictus> Ric<ard>us Wakefeild in p<ro>pr<ia> p<er>sona sua et cepit de D<omi>no
man<er>ij p<re>d<icti> omnia et sing<u>la p<re>miss<a> p<re>d<icta> cui D<omi>n<us>
p<re>d<ictus> p<er> cl<er>ic<u>m suu<m> p<re>d<ictum> concessit inde sei<sin>am p<er> virgam
s<e>c<un>d<u>m consuetud<inem> man<er>ij p<re>d<icti> h<ab>end<um> et tenend<um>
p<re>missa p<re>d<icta> p<re>fat<o> Ric<ard>o Wakefeild hered<ibus> et assign<atis> suis
im<per>p<et>uu<m> ad voluntat D<omi>ni s<e>c<un>d<u>m consuetud<inem> man<er>ij
p<re>d<icti> p<ro> Reddit<ibus> et servic<iis> inde prius debit<is> et de jure consuetud' et dat
D<omi>ino man<er>ij p<re>d<icti> p<ro> fine ad ingr<essu>m duodecim denar<ios> et p<ost> tres
p<ro>clam<ationes> inde fact<as> s<e>c<un>d<u>m consuetud<ine>m man<er>ij p<re>d<icti> fecit
D<omi>no fidelitat et admissus est inde tenens

Manor of Tutbury. Small court of the lord king of England held at Tutbury for the aforesaid
manor on the 19th day of January in the 2nd year of the reign of our lord James II now king
of England, etc., [1687] before Edward Foden, clerk there, in the presence of Henry
Harlowe and George Harlowe customary tenants of the aforesaid manor.
To this court came Samuel Emery father and Samuel Emery son of the same Samuel the
father, in their own persons, and surrendered into the hands of the lord of the aforesaid
manor by the rod according to the custom of the aforesaid manor a messuage or tenement
with appurtenances and two parcels of land next to Belmote Lane commonly called Poole
Milne Croft and Tippers Riddings, within the manor of Tutbury aforesaid, with all and
singular their appurtenances to the use and behoof of Richard Wakefeild, gentleman, his
heirs and assigns for ever, at the will of the lord according to the custom of the aforesaid
manor and so it remains in the hands of the lord of the aforesaid manor and on this into this
and the same court came the aforesaid Richard Wakefeild in his own person and received
from the lord of the aforesaid manor all and singular the aforesaid premises, to whom the
aforesaid lord by his clerk aforesaid granted thence seisin by the rod according to the custom
of the aforesaid manor, to have and to hold the aforesaid premises to the aforesaid Richard
Wakefeild his heirs and assigns for ever at the will of the lord according to the custom of the
aforesaid manor for the rent and services thence formerly due and by right accustomed, and
he gives to the lord of the aforesaid manor for a fine at his entry 12d. And after three
proclamations thence made according to the custom of the aforesaid manor he did fealty to
the lord and was admitted thence tenant.

Example 14 (p. 39)

Ad cur<iam> eiusd<e>m tent<am> ib<ide>m die m<er>cur<ii> p<ro>x<imo> post f<estu>m S<anc>ti Pet<ri> Ap<osto>li A<nn>o r<egni> r<egis> Henrici sept<imi> quinto Jur<atores> ex offic<i>o videl<i>c<e>t Will<eb>m<u>s Shepp<er>d Thom<a>s Shepp<er>d Will<elmu>s Chaplen Will<elmu>s Makley Joh<ann>es Mason filius Will<elm>i Andreas Busby Ric<ardus> Yo<u>ng Thomas Whornby Ric<ardus> Chapleyn Will<elmu>s Hiklyng Henricus Brown et Thom<a>s Orchard Jur<ati> present<ant> q<uod> Thom<a>s Wyn<ne> qui tenuit de d<omi>no duo crofta vocat<a> Pole Myln Croft et Typper Rydding p<er> copiam secundum cons<uetudinem> Man<er>ij mortuus est Et nichil accidit d<omi>no post eius decessu<m> Et q<uod> Joh<ann>es Wynne est heres eiusd Thome dict<is> croft<is> hereditizand<is> s<e>c<un>d<u>m Cons<uetudinem> Man<er>ij ib<ide>m Ideo p<ost>ea p<re>c<eptum> est Ball<ivio> q<uod> seis<et> dict<a> croft<a> in manus d<omi>ni qu<o>sq<ue> etc. Et sup<er> hoc ven<it> p<re>dict<us> Joh<ann>es Wyn<ne> in eade<m> cur<ia> et cepit de d<omi>no predict<a> croft<a> tenend<a> sibi her<edibus> et assign<atis> suis s<e>c<un>d<u>m Cons<uetudinem> Man<er>ij reddend<o> inde p<er> annu<m> reddit<us> s<er>vicia et Cons<uetudines> inde debit<a> et Cons<ueta> Et dat d<omi>no de fine ad ingressum xijd. Et admiss<us> est Tenens et fecit fidelitat
De Tempore Jacobi Blount Milit<is> Capital<is> Senesc<alli> honoris de Tutbur<y>

At the court of the same held there on Wednesday next after the feast of Saint Peter the Apostle in the 5th year of the reign of King Henry VII [30 June 1490] the jurors by virtue of their office namely, William Shepperd, Thomas Shepperd, William Chaplen, William Makley, John Mason son of William, Andrew Busby, Richard Young, Thomas Whornby, Richard Chapleyn, William Hiklyng, Henry Brown, and Thomas Orchard, sworn, present that Thomas Wynne who held of the lord two crofts called Pole Myln Croft and Typper Rydding by copy according to the custom of the manor has died and nothing falls due to the lord after his death. And that John Wynne is the heir of the same Thomas to the said crofts to be inherited according to the custom of the manor there. Therefore afterwards the bailiff was ordered to take the said crofts into the hands of the lord until etc. And on this the aforesaid John Wynne came into the same court and received the aforesaid crofts from the lord, to hold to him, his heirs and assigns according to the custom of the manor, rendering thence annually the rents, services and customs thence owed and accustomed. And he gives to the lord for a fine at [his] entry 12d. and was admitted tenant and did fealty.
From the time of James Blount, knight, chief steward of the Honour of Tutbury.

Example 15 (p. 39)

Qui quidem Jur<atores> on<er>at<i> et jur<ati> de et sup<er> articulis hunc visum tangent<ibus> dic<u>nt sup<er> s<a>cr<a>m<ent>a sua q<uo>d Georgi<us> (iiijd.) Greysley miles heres <ijd.> Thome Bagot defuncti iam infra etatem et in custodia Reg<is> existens Joh<ann>es (iiijd.) Mytton Ar<miger> Joh<ann>es (iiijd.) Wollsley ar<miger>, capellanus <iiijd.> cantarie de Kingeley Thom<a>s (iid.) Puleson Rich<ard>us (ijd.) Glasson Rich<ard>us <ijd.> Waken de Rassleston et Thom<a>s (ijd.) Pereson debent sect<am> cur<ie> et non vener<u>nt Et ordinat<um> est p<er> jur<atores> p<re>dict<os> q<uo>d nullus tenent<iarius> ib<ide>m p<er>mittet ullum aliu<m> tenent<iarium> secu<m> cohabitare in domo sua post fest<um> Nativitat<is> s<an>cti Joh<ann>is Baptiste p<ro>x<imum> futur<um> sub pena iijs. (?) iiijd. Et q<uo>d quilib<e>t tenent<iariorum> p<re>dict<orum> faciet sepes suas circa ca<m>pos seminat<os> p<ra>ta et clausuras ante d<om>in<i>cam terciam Quadrigesime sub pena cui<us>lib<e>t rupture no<n> fact<e> xijd. et cui<us>lib<e>t defect<us> vjd. et ulteri<us> dic<u>nt q<uo>d Will<eb>m<us> Snape (xijd.) vendit carnes insalubres infra d<o>min<i>um p<re>dict<um> in p<re>iudici<u>m sanitatis o<mn>i<u>m tenent<iariorum> ib<ide>m et ult<ra> o<mn>ia b<e>n<e>

Which jurors charged and sworn concerning and on the articles touching this view say on their oaths that George Greysley (4d.) knight, the heir (2d.) of Thomas Bagot deceased, now under age and being in the wardship of the king, John Mytton, (4d.) esquire, John Wollsley (4d.) esquire, the chaplain of the chantry of Kingley, Thomas Puleson (2d.), Richard Glasson (2d.), Richard Waken of Rosliston (2d.), and Thomas Pereson (2d.) owe suit of court and have not come. And it is ordered by the aforesaid jurors that no tenant there shall allow any other tenant to live with him in his house after the feast of the Nativity of Saint John the Baptist next to come under penalty of 3s. 4d. And that each aforesaid tenant shall make his hedges about the sown fields, meadows and closes before the third Sunday in Lent under penalty for each gap not filled up 12d. and for each default 6d. and further they say that William Snape (12d.) sells rotten meat within the aforesaid demesne to the danger of the health of all the tenants there and otherwise all is well.

Example 16 (p. 41)

Qui quidem Jurat<i> p<re>d<i>c<t>i sup<er> sacr<a>m<entum> suu<m> dic<unt> q<uo>d Joh<ann>es Fuller (xijd.) p<ar>cum fregit communem Ideoq<ue> ip<s>e in m<isericord>ia p<ro>ut etc. Item insup<er> sup<er> sacr<a>m<ent>um p<re>d<i>c<t>u<m> dic<unt> q<uo>d Tho<mas> vjd. Porter Will<elmu>s (iiijd.) Wrighson Tho<mas> (iiijd.) Hall Anth<oni>us <iiijd.> Kinge Will<elmu>s Anderson (iiijd.) transgr<essi> sunt et quil<ibe>t eor<um> trans<gressus> est cu<m> av<er>ijs suis in quod<am> loco vocat<o> Braygate feilde Ideoq<ue> ip<s>i et eor<um> quil<ibe>t in m<isericord>ia p<ro>ut etc. Item dicunt q<uo>d Rob<er>tus (vjd.) Doddes effodit ex le becke anglice hathe cutte out of the becke et p<er>misit aquam decurrere quand<am> venella<m> vocat<am> Boston laine Ideoq<ue> ip<s>e in m<isericord>ia p<ro>ut etc.

Which aforesaid jurors on oath say that John Fuller (12d.) broke [into] the common park and therefore he is in mercy as etc. Likewise moreover upon [their] aforesaid oath they say that Thomas (6d.) Porter, William (4d.) Wrighson, Thomas (4d.) Hall, Anthony (4d.) Kinge, William (4d.) Anderson trespassed and each of them trespassed with their beasts in a certain place called Braygate Field and therefore they and each of them [are] in mercy as etc.
Likewise they say that Robert (6d.) Doddes dug out of the becke in English 'hathe cutte out of the becke' and allowed the water to flow down a certain lane called Boston Lane and therefore he [is] in mercy as etc.

Example 17 (p. 41)

Cur<ia> de Alrewas tent<a> die sabb<at>i post f<estu>m s<anc>ti Sedde epi<scopi> a<nn>o r<egni> r<egis> E<dwardi> t<er>tij post <con>quest<um> xlvj° Ric<ardus> fil<ius> Joh<ann>is Baxt<er> venit i<n> plena cur<ia> et sursu<m> reddit in manu d<omi>ni unu<m> cot<agium> cu<m> p<er>tin<entiis> in Alrewas una cu<m> al<iis> t<e>r<ris> et ten<ementis> cu<m> p<er>tin<entiis> que tenet in eadem ac cu<m> rev<er>t<i>o<n>e di<midiam> acr<am> t<er>r<e> q<uo>d Matilda Orbeby (?) tenet in dote salvo d<ic>to Ric<ard>o una placea uni<us> furm<e> Et postea sursu<m> reddit p<re>dict<a>m plac<eam> furm<e> ad op<us> Henr<ici> Adkok et Matild<e> ux<or>is ei<us> ad tota<m> vita<m> sua<m> tenend<am> p<er> s<er>vic<ia> p<ri>us inde debita

Court of Alrewas held on Saturday after the feast of Saint Chad the bishop in the 46th year of the reign of king Edward III after the conquest [6 March 1372]. Richard son of John Baxter comes in full court and surrenders into the hand of the lord one cottage with appurtenances in Alrewas together with other lands and tenements with appurtenances which he holds in the same and with the reversion of a half acre of land which Matilda Orbeby (?) holds in dowry saving to the said Richard one plot of one farm. And afterwards he surrenders the aforesaid plot of farm to the use of Henry Adkok and Matilda his wife to hold for all his life by the services thence formerly owed.

Example 18 (p. 41)

Q<ue>rela Int<er> Will<elmu>m Owen <con>q<ue>rente<m> et Will<elmu>m p<re>po<s>itu<m>
defend<entem> In r<espect>u usq<ue> cur<iam> p<ro>x<ima>m
Nich<olaus> le Blund dist<ri>ng<itur> p<ro> sua defalta ad magna<m> cur<iam> et et<iam> q<uia>
ess<oniavit> se ad magna<m> et no<n> ad s<e>c<un>d<a>m warantizavit
Henr<icus> Av<er>il In m<isericord>ia p<ro> q<ue>rela mota de q<ua>da<m> semita apud
Oreg<ra>ve
Tota t<er>ra Rob<ert>i fil<ii> Reginald<i> saysiat<ur> In manu d<omi>ni cu<m> tota west<ur>a
p<ro> sua m<isericord>ia It Rob<ertus> Aylm<er> de Alrewas In manu d<omi>ni lib<er>avit et
om<n>ino coram plena cur<ia> de ead abiuravit totam t<er>ram suam scilic<et> unam virgatam
cu<m> p<er>tinentiis q<ua>m tenuit In Alrewas de h<er>editat<e> sua

The suit between William Owen plaintiff and William the reeve defendant is respited until
the next court.
Nicholas le Blund is distrained for his default at the great court and also because he essoined
himself at the great [court] and did not warrant [himself] at the second [court].
Henry Averil [is] in mercy for a suit instituted concerning a certain lane in Orgrave.
All the land of Robert son of Reginald is taken into the hand of the lord with all crops for his
fine.
Likewise Robert Aylmer of Alrewas delivered into the hand of the lord and before the full
court of the same [place] entirely renounced on oath all his land, namely one virgate with
appurtenances which he held in Alrewas by his inheritance.

Exercise 12 (p. 43)

(a) Rental made and renewed by the oath of John Blounte and Arthur Meverell on the 20
     April 1573 and in the 15th year of the reign of our lady Elizabeth.

(b) William son of Henry Lug holds a tenement formerly belonging to William his
     grandfather paying 6d.

(c) Richard of Potlak carpenter holds one burgage by right of Ellen his wife paying to the
     abbot 12d.

(d) John of London holds one cottage and one acre of land which used to render annually
     3s. 6d. now 2s.

(e) Alice of Stafford holds tenements lately belonging to Benedict Mountgomery and
     renders annually at Pentecost term 4d. or one pound of cumin.

(f) Ralph Leysing villein holds one messuage and one virgate of land lately belonging to
     Richard Leysing and renders annually at the terms of Martinmas and the Nativity of
     John the Baptist 3s. 6d.

(g) The same Ralph must mow in the lord's meadows for one day at his own expense and
     gives for the same work 4d.

(h) ... and he will make hay [for one] day a year and will reap in autumn for three days and
     he will plough for one day at the winter sowing and at the Lent [i.e. spring] sowing.

Exercise 13 (p. 44)

(a) *Ad<am> de Neuton t<enet> burg<agium> q<uo>nda<m> Joh<ann>is Penifot de iur<e> Marg<er>ie ux<oris> sue solv<endo> iiijd.*

Adam of Neuton holds a burgage formerly belonging to John Penifot by right of Margery his wife paying 4d.

(b) *Joh<ann>es Lugg ten<et> di<midiam> acr<am> t<er>re árabilis et redd<it> p<er> annu<m> xvjd.*

John Lugg holds a half acre of arable land and renders annually 16d.

(c) *Will<elmu>s le Park<er> t<enet> un<um> mess<uagium> cu<m> p<er>tin<entiis> redd<endo> e<isdem> t<erminis> xxd.*

William the parker holds one messuage with appurtenances paying at the same terms 20d.

(d) *D<omi>n<u>s Th<oma>s de Aldelu<m> capell<anu>s t<enet> ad t<erminu>m vite sue un<am> acr<am> et di<midium> et redd<it> vjd.*

Sir Thomas of Audlem, chaplain, holds for the term of his life one acre and a half and pays 6d.

(e) *Alic<ia> fil<ia> Rad<ulph>i Baron ten<et> al<terum> di<midium> d<i>c<t>i ten<ementi> de dono patr<is> sui et reddit vjd.*

Alice daughter of Ralph Baron holds the other half of the said tenement by gift of her father and pays 6d.

(f) *Galf<ridus> pist<or> t<enet> q<ua>md<am> plac<eam> q<uo>nd<am> J<ohannis> f<rat>ris sui*

Geoffrey the baker holds a certain plot formerly belonging to John his brother.

(g) *Elena fil<ia> Walt<er>i tinctor<is> tenet un<am> parcell<am> prati iuxta Skyrem<er> medwe et extendit se ex t<ra>v<er>so ad alt<am> viam*

Ellen the daughter of Walter the dyer holds a parcel of meadow next to Skyremer meadow and it extends across to the highway.

Example 19 (p. 47)
Brameley in Com<itatu> Stafford<ie>. Liber<ri> redd<itus> burg<agiorum> de Brameley.
Joh<ann>es Bardell tenet lib<er>e iiij<uor> burg<agia> cu<m> p<er>tin<entiis> ~~et reddit p<er> annu<m>~~ Solvend<o> ad f<estum> s<anc>ti Martini in hieme tu<nc> p<er> annu<m> iiijs.
Hugo Bussell tenet lib<ere> div<er>sa burg<agia> et ~~redd<it> inde~~ sol<vendo> eod t<erm>ino p<er> annu<m> vjs.xd.
Rob<er>tus Bank<es> tenet burg<agium> cu<m> p<er>tin<entiis> et Reddit p<er> annu<m> ijs.vjd.
Joh<ann>es Bate tenet duob<us> burg<agia> cu<m> p<er>tin<entiis> et reddit p<er> annu<m> iijs.vjd.

Bromley in the County of Stafford. Free rents of burgages of Bromley.

John Bardell holds freely 4 burgages with appurtenances and renders annually *(crossed through)* paying at the feast of Saint Martin in Winter ... annually 4s.

Hugh Bussell holds freely various burgages and renders thence *(crossed through)* paying at the same term annually 6s. 10d.

Robert Bankes holds a burgage with appurtenances and renders annually 2s. 6d.

John Bate holds 2 burgages with appurtenances and renders annually 3s. 6d.

Example 20 (p. 47)

Tenen<tes> p<er> copiam

Robert<us> Browne tenet unu<m> mess<uagium> cu<m> p<er>tin<entiis> et Reddit p<er> Annu<m> xvijs.

Joh<an>nes Harvye tenet unu<m> mess<uagium> cu<m> p<er>tin<entiis> et Reddit p<er> Annu<m> xxijs.iijd.

Will<el>m<u>s Harvye tenet unu<m> mess<uagium> cu<m> p<er>tin<entiis> et reddit p<er> Annu<m> xxs.vjd.

Joh<an>nes Arnolde tenet unu<m> mess<uagium> cu<m> p<er>tin<entiis> et reddit p<er> Annu<m> xxviijs

Edmundus hall tenet unu<m> mess<uagium> cu<m> p<er>tin<entiis> et reddit p<er> Annu<m> xxixs.iiijd.

Tenants by copy.

Robert Browne holds one messuage with appurtenances and pays annually 17s.

John Harvye holds one messuage with appurtenances and pays annually 22s. 3d. (English in margin 'his copie is in Worcettshire,)

William Harvye holds one messuage with appurtenances and pays annually 20s. 6d.

John Arnolde holds one messuage with appurtenances and pays annually 28s.

Edmund Hall holds one messuage with appurtenances and pays annually 29s. 4d.

Example 21 (p. 49)

Terr<e> d<o>m<in>ical<es> de bramley

Joh<ann>es Bardell tenet cert<as> p<ar>cell<as> terra<rum> d<om>inical<ium> et Reddit p<er> Annu<m> xiijs.iiijd.

Thom<a>s Hyron et Joh<ann>es Alporte tene<n>t c<er>t<as> p<ar>cell<as> Terra<rum> d<o>m<in>ical<ium> et reddu<n>t p<er> Annu<m> xiijs.iiijd.

Demesne lands of Bromley

John Bardell holds certain parcels of demesne lands and pays annually 13s. 4d.

Thomas Hyron and John Alporte hold certain parcels of demesne lands and pay annually 13s. 4d.

Example 22 (p. 51)

D<omi>n<u>s Th<oma>s de Aldelu<m> capell<anu>s t<enet> ad t<erminu>m vite sue et W. f<rat>ris sui j. burg<agium> et di<midium> de J. le Knyttesone q<uo>nd<am> Ric<ardi> textor<is> <solvendo> abb<at>i xviijd.

Elena fil<ia> G. Prudfot t<enet> iij burg<agia> iur<e> her<editario> solv<endo> abb<at>i iijs.

Rosa Prudfot t<enet> ij burg<agia> de dono mag<ist>ri W. de henov<er>e que fu<eru>nt q<uo>nd<am> J. Prudfot solv<endo> abb<at>i ij sol<idos>

Ad<am> de Neuton' t<enet> iiij burg<agia> de iure marg<er>ie ux<oris> sue que fueru<n>t q<uo>nd<am> Rob<ert>i hadcote q<uorum> duo fueru<n>t q<uo>nd<am> J. Walraund et duo J. d<i>c<t>i prest solv<endo> abb<at>i iiijs.

Ric<ardus> fil<ius> Alani cirotecar<ij> t<enet> iij burg<agia> et di<midium> iur<e> hered<itario> solv<endo> abb<at>i iijs.vjd.

Sir Thomas de Aldelum chaplain holds for the term of his life and of W. his brother one burgage and a half of J. of Knyttesone, formerly belonging to Richard the weaver, [paying] to the abbot 18d.

Ellen daughter of G. Prudfot holds three burgages by hereditary right paying to the abbot 3s.

Rosa Prudfot holds two burgages by gift of Master W. of Heanor which formerly belonged to J. Prudfot paying to the abbot 2s.

Adam of Neuton holds four burgages by right of Margery his wife formerly belonging to Robert Hadcote of which two formerly belonged to J. Walraund and two to J. called the priest, paying to the abbot 4s.

Richard son of Alan the glover holds three burgages and a half by hereditary right paying to the abbot 3s. 6d.

Example 23 (p. 51)

Rent<a>le ib<ide>m fact<um> et renovat<um> p<er> quand<a>m sup<erv>is<ionem> inde fact<um> xxiiij<to> August<i> 1579 et A<nn>o regni d<omi>ne n<ost>re Elizabeth<e> Regine etc. xxj(mo)
Lychfeilde Streete
From watsons house on the north syde of Lychfeld st<reete> untill yo<u> come into halfe streete
Ric<ard>us watson tenet lib<er>e de d<omi>no un<um> ten<emen>t<um> cu<m> gardino cont<inens> un<am> Rod<am> et borealit<er> abbutt<ans> sup<er> claus<uram> sive croft<um> ~~Tho~~ <me> Will<el>mi Watson et cognovit se reddere ann<uatim> p<ro> p<re>miss<i>s ijs.
Rob<er>t<us> Richardson cognovit se tenere ad volunt<atem> un<um> cotag<ium> cu<m> gardin<o> cont<inens> di<midiam> Rod<am> et abb<uttans> boreal<iter> sup<er> claus<uram> p<re>d<ictam> et redd<it> p<er> Ann<um> vs.
Will<el>m<u>s watson tenet p<er> Indentur<am> dat<am> x<imo> Aprilis A<nn>o xxj<mo> d<omi>ne Elizabeth<e> Reg<ine> unu<m> ten<emen>t<um> m<od>o in duob<us> ten<emen>t<is> devis<i>s ac duo croft<a> eisd<e>m adiacen<tia> cont<inentia> p<er> Estimat<ionem> unu<m> Rod<am> et abbutt<antia> ut sup<ra> et redd<it> p<er> Ann<um> xs.
Matheus Smythe cognovit se tenere ad volunt<atem> duo gardin<a> cont<inentia> p<er> estimat<ionem> di<midiam> Rod<am> et abb<uttantia> ut sup<ra> et redd<it> p<er> Ann<um> xxd.
   S<um> m<a> xviijs.viijd.

Rental there made and renewed by a certain survey thence made 24 August 1579 and in the 21st year of the reign of our Lady Elizabeth Queen etc.

Lichfield Street.

(English not repeated)

Richard Watson holds freely of the lord one tenement with a garden containing one rood and abutting to the north on a close or croft of Tho [mas] *(crossed through)* William Watson and he acknowledges that he pays annually for the premises 2s.

Robert Richardson acknowledges that he holds at will one cottage with a garden containing a half rood and abutting to the north on the aforesaid close and he pays annually 5s.

William Watson holds by indenture dated 10 April in the 21st year of the Lady Queen Elizabeth one tenement now divided into two tenements and two crofts adjoining the same containing by estimation one rood and abutting as above and he pays annually 10s.

Matthew Smythe acknowledges that he holds at will two gardens containing by estimation a half rood and abutting as above and he pays annually 20d.

   Sum total 18s. 8d.

Example 24 (p. 53)

Rentale de la hurste renovatu<m> et factu<m> p<er> sacr<a>m<entum> Will<elm>i hurne et Will<elm>i good t<u>nc collector<es> coram Joh<ann>e Sudb<er>y t<un>c abb<a>te ad festu<m> pasch<e> anno eiusd<e>m abb<a>t<is> xvj<o> et anno Regni Reg<is> Henr<ici> q<u>inti quarto

Alicia Dycon t<enet> vj acr<as> t<er>r<e> in brereleyfeld q<uon>d<a>m Will<elm>i Brokholes r<eddendo> p<er> a<nnum> ad t<erminos> s<an>c<t>i mart<in>i et Nati<vi>tat<is> s<an>c<t>i Joh<ann>is Bapt<ist>e iiijs.vj.

Ead<e>m Alic<ia> te<net> tres acr<as> t<er>r<e> i<n> Brounefeld q<uon>d<a>m si<mi>lit<er> d<i>c<t>i Will<elm>i r<eddendo> p<er> a<nnum> e<isdem> t<erminis> ijs.

Her<vey> del boty te<net> un<am> acr<am> j rod<am> t<er>r<e> nup<er> Will<elm>i Rede i<n> feodo de bagot r<eddendo> e<isdem> t<erminis> ijs.

Joh<anne>s molle t<enet> acr<am> t<er>r<e> voc<ate> taylo<r>feld nup<er> isold<e> ha<r>v<e>y r<eddendo> p<er> a<nnum> e<isdem> t<erminis> iijs.

Id<e>m Joh<anne>s t<enet> iij rod<as> t<er>r<e> in brereleyhay voc<ate> taylo<r> crofte r<eddendo> e<isdem> t<erminis> ixd.

Rob<er>tus Turne<r> t<enet> iiij acr<as> et di<midium> t<er>r<e> voc<ate> le Trench nup<er> Will<elm>i good r<eddendo> ijs.iijd.

Rental of the Hurst renewed and made on the oath of William Hurne and William Good then collectors before John Sudbury then abbot at the feast of Easter in the 16th year of the same abbot and in the 4th year of the reign of King Henry V (Easter 1416)

Alice Dycon holds six acres of land in Brereleyfield formerly belonging to William Brokholes paying annually at the terms of Saint Martin and the Nativity of Saint John the Baptist 4s. 6d.

The same Alice holds three acres of land in Brounefield formerly similarly belonging to the said William, paying annually at the same terms 2s.

Hervey del Boty holds one acre one rood of land formerly belonging to William Rede in fee of Bagot, paying at the same terms 2s.

John Molle holds an acre of land called Taylorfield formerly belonging to Isolda Harvey, paying annually at the same terms 3s.

The same John holds three roods of land in Brereleyhay called Taylor Croft, paying at the same terms 9d.

Robert Turner holds four acres and a half of land called Le Trench formerly belonging to William Good, paying 2s. 3d.

Example 25 (p. 55)

Lib<erati>o redd<itus> exeunt<is> de uno mes<suagio> cum p<er>tinen<tiis> ib<ide>m Will<elm>i hethecote p<er> Annu<m> iiijs.vjd.

Lib<erati>o redd<itus> exeunt<is> de div<ersi>s p<ar>cell<is> terr<e> ib<ide>m Joh<an>nis Norton p<er> Annu<m> xjd.

Lib<erati>o redd<itus> exeunt<is> de Terr<a> Joh<an>nis Blounte ib<ide>m p<er> Annu<m> iiijd.

Lib<erati>o redd<itus> exeunt<is> de Terr<a> Arthuri mev<er>ell ib<ide>m p<er> annu<m> jd. ob<olum>   vs.xd.ob<olum>

Reddit<us> Terr<e> ib<ide>m dimiss<e> Joh<an>ni Buste ad voluntat d<omi>ni de Anno in Annu<m> Reddend<o> inde p<er> Annu<m> viijd.

Redd<itus> unius mes<suagij> ib<ide>m dimiss<i> hered<ibus> Edwardi Proudeholme ad volunt<atem> d<omi>ni Reddend<o> inde p<er> Annu<m> ixs.iiijd.   xs.

Reddit<us> sive Firma unius mes<suagij> necnon om<n>i<um> prato<rum> pascua<rum> et pastur<e> eid<e>m p<er>tinen<tium> dimiss<i> Joh<an>ni hallam p<er> Copiam Cur<ie> dat<am> xxij° die maij Anno r<egni> r<egis> henr<ici> viij(vi)xxxviij° h<ab>end<um> sibi p<ro> t<er>mi<n>o vite sue s<e>c<un>d<u>m cons<uetudinem> man<er>ij ib<ide>m p<er> Annu<m> xvijs. viijd.

Redd<itus> sive Firma unius mes<suagij> ib<ide>m cum x(is) Feni d<i>c<t>i mes<suagij> dimiss<i>
Will<el>mo harrison p<er> Copiam Cur<ie> dat<am> die et Anno p<re>d<icto> h<ab>end<um> sibi
Johanne ux<or>i eius   xvijs. viiijd.

Payment of rent issuing from one messuage with appurtenances there belonging to William
Hethecote annually 4s. 6d.
Payment of rent issuing from various parcels of land there belonging to John Norton
annually 11d.
Payment of rent issuing from the land of John Blounte there annually 4d.
Payment of rent issuing from the land of Arthur Meverell there annually 1d.   5s. 10d.
Rent of land there demised to John Buste at the will of the lord from year to year paying
thence annually 8d.
Rent of one messuage there demised to the heirs of Edward Proudeholme at the will of the
lord paying thence annually 9s. 4d.   10s.
Rent or farm of one messuage and also of all meadows, pastures and rights of pasture
pertaining to the same demised to John Hallam by copy of the court [roll] dated 22nd day of
May in the 38th year of the reign of King Henry VIII to hold to him for the term of his life
according to the custom of the manor there annually 17s. 8d.
Rent or farm of one messuage there with the (tenths) of hay of the said messuage demised to
William Harrison by copy of court [roll] dated the day and year aforesaid to hold to him,
[and] Joan his wife   17s. 8d.

Example 26 (p. 57)

brytheston Extent<a> man<er>ii prior<is> de Okeborn' de Brytheston' f<ac>ta die Nativitat<is> be<ate>
mar<ie> anno r<egni> r<egis> E<dwardi> xxij° p<er> Joh<anne>m de Sunninges Will<elmu>m de
molend<ino> Joh<annem> le boteler Will<elmum> Stiward Joh<annem> Esmond Will<elmum>
Wyneband Joh<annem> de Witecline Joh<annem> Le ku Joh<annem> maynard Godefr<idum> morys
Rob<er>t<um> Symond et Ph<illipu>m le Swon jur<atores> qui d<icu>nt q<uo>d Cur<ia> ibid
cu<m> gardino et uno columbar<io> val<et> p<er> annu<m> xiijs. iiijd. It redd<unt> villan<i>
p<er> annu<m> iiij li. vjs. It s<er>vic<ia> et op<er>at<iones> custumar<ie> vale<n>t p<er>
annu<m> x li.iiijs.ixd. It d<icu>nt q<uo>d su<n>t xxiij villani in univ<er>so et poss<u>nt
sem<e>l talliar<i> p<er> annu<m> p<ro> voluntate d<omi>ni It d<icu>nt q<uo>d plac<ita> et
p<er>quis<ita> cu<m> finib<us> t<er>r<e> vale<n>t p<er> annu<m> vjs.viijd. It d<icu>nt
q<uo>d sunt in man<er>io Dccxvij acr<e> t<er>re arab<ilis> et val<et> quel<ibet> acr<a> p<er>
annu<m> iiijd. It d<icu>nt q<uo>d s<u>nt vj acr<e> p<ra>ti q<uarum> quel<ibet> val<et> p<er>
annu<m> ijs. It d<icu>nt q<uo>d pastur<a> man<er>ii val<et> p<er> annu<m> xljs.
S<um>m<a> xxj li. ixd.

Brixton Extent of the manor of the prior of Ogbourne of Brixton made on the day of the
nativity of the Blessed Mary in the 22nd year of the reign of king Edward [8th September
1294] by John de Sunninges, William of the mill, John le Butler, William Stiward, John
Esmond, William Wyneband, John de Witecline, John le Ku, John Maynard Godfrey Morys,
Robert Symond and Phillip le Swon, jurors, who say that the house there with garden
and one dovecote is worth 13s. 4d. annually. Likewise the villeins pay annually £4 6s. Likewise
the services and customary works are worth annually £10 4s. 9d. Likewise they say that
there are 23 villeins in all and they can be tallaged once a year at the will of the lord.
Likewise they say that the pleas and profits <of the court> with the fines of land are worth
6s. 8d. annually. Likewise they say that there are in the manor 717 acres of arable land, and
each acre is worth 4d. a year. Likewise they say that there are 6 acres of meadow of which
each acre is worth 2s. annually. Likewise they say that the pasture of the manor is worth
41s. annually. Total £21 0s. 9d.

Exercise 14 (p. 59)

(a) Ralph reeve of Barton renders account of £8 12½d. from the morrow of Saint Michael.

(b) Account of William Clapbroke reeve there, from the feast of Saint Michael in the third year of king Edward IV to the same feast of Saint Michael then following in the fourth year of the same king, namely for one whole year.

(c) And of £6 5s. 5d. of fixed rent from the term of the Annunciation.

(d) The same renders account of 21s. 8d. of dayworks and customs sold.

(e) Issues of the manor. The same renders account of 2s. 5d. revenue from the pannage of pigs of the lord's tenants ... and of 5s. revenue from eight cocks and six hens sold.

(f) Rent of the fishing. And of 13s. for the rent of the fishing of the water of Foxford.

(g) Profits of the court. And of 9s. 7d. of profits of two views [i.e. of frankpledge] held there

(h) Sum total of receipts with arrears £41 9s. 5¼d.

Example 27 (p. 61)

Compot<us> Gilb<er>ti Bulluc p<re>po<si>ti de Berlinh<a>m a festo s<an>c<t>i Gregor<ii> p<ap>e anno r<egni> r<egis> Edwardi fil<ii> reg<is> Henr<ici> q<ua>rto usq<ue> purificat<i>onem be<ate> marie p<ro>x<imam> seq<uentem>

Account of Gilbert Bulluc reeve of Berlinham from the feast of Saint Gregory the pope in the 4th year of the reign of king Edward son of king Henry [12 March 1276], to the Purification of the Blessed Mary next following [2 February].

Example 28 (p. 61) ·

Idem r<eddit> comp<otum> de ijs.vd. r<eceptis> de pannag<io> porco<rum> ten<entium> d<omi>ni et de vs. r<eceptis> de gland<iis> vend<itis> et de xxvs.jd. r<eceptis> de pastur<a> vend<ita> et de iiijs. r<eceptis> de p<ra>to vend<ito> Et de ixd. r<eceptis> de bruar<i> vend<it>i Et de ijs. r<eceptis> de sirp<is> vend<itis> et de xxd. r<eceptis> de forag<io> vend<ito>
    S<um> m<a> xls.xjd.

The same renders account of 2s. 5d. received from the pannage of pigs of the lord's tenants and of 5s. received from the sale of acorns and of 25s. 1d. received from the sale of pasture and of 4s. received from the sale of meadow and of 9d. received from the sale of heath and of 2s. received from the sale of rushes and of 20d. received from the sale of fodder. Total 40s. 11d.

Example 29 (p. 61)

Onus Joh<an>nis Godwyne Ballivi ib<ide>m In Anno Regine Eliz<abethe> iij<cio>
De Arr<eragiis> ult<imi> Comp<ot>i nulla q<uia> prius comp<ut>us
De Reddit<ibus> assis<is> sive Lib<eris> Reddit<ibus> Burg<i> ib<ide>m p<er> Annu<m> viij li. vijs.jd.
De Reddit<ibus> nup<er> p<er>tinen<tis> Guilde ib<ide>m p<er> An<nu>m clare ultra vs.ijd. Lxxs.iiijd.
De p<er>quis<iti>s Cur<ie> ib<ide>m hoc Anno xxxjs.iijd.
De vendic<i>one Bosco<rum> ib<ide>m vend<itorum> hoc A<nn>o xls.
    ~~xiij li. viijs. viijd.~~   xvi li. vijs.viijd.   De Om<ni>bus
In den<ar>ijs lib<er>at<is> ad manus Ric<ard>i Cupp<er> xviij[dg] Ap<ri>lis Anno iij(cio) Eliz<abethe> Cxviijs. viijd.

Ed ad manus d<i>c<t>i Ric<ardi> Cupper iij<cio> die Novembr<is> 1561 iiij li. xvijs. xd.
   xli. xvjs. vjd.

Charge on John Godwyne bailiff there in the 3rd year of Queen Elizabeth.
For arrears from the last account none because already accounted.
For fixed rents or free rents of the borough there annually £8 7s. 1d.
For rents formerly belonging to the Gild there annually net above 5s. 2d.
72s. 4d.
For profits of the court there this year 31s. 3d.
For sales of wood sold there this year 40s.
£13 8s. 8d. *(crossed through)*   £16 8s. 8d.   for all
For monies delivered into the hands of Richard Cupper 18 April in the 3rd year of Elizabeth
£5 18s. 8d.
And to the hands of the said Richard Cupper 3rd day November 1561 £4 17s. 10d.
£40 16s. 6d.

Exercise 15 (p. 63)
(a)   William of Shobnall holds two bovates for 2s. and must go wherever he is sent.

(b)   The dyer has two bovates for 2s. 6d. and must lend his plough twice a year and mow
      three times in August in two places with one man [and a] third [time] with all his men
      with food provided by the lord.

(c)   Each villein holds two bovates and works two days in the week ... and owes two hens at
      Christmas ... and pays pannage and ploughs twice in the year and besides this in Lent
      half an acre and from Pentecost to the feast of All Saints he sends his animals into the
      lord's foldyard.

(d)   The same shall perform various carrying and carting services of food and other
      necessaries of the lord whenever he shall have been summoned and he gives for each
      customary service 2s. 10d. annually.

(e)   ... and he must pay tallage for each year with his neighbours at the feast of Saint Martin.

Exercise 16 (p. 64)
(a)   *Et q<ue>libet septimana op<er>abili a p<re>d<i>c<t>o festo usq<ue> ad festu<m> s<an>c<t>i
      Pet<ri> ad vinc<u>la debet op<er>ari p<er> t<re>s dies q<ua>l<iter>cu<m>q<ue> d<omi>n<u>s
      voluerit*

And each week of works from the aforesaid feast to the feast of Saint Peter in Chains he must
work for three days at whatever work the lord shall have wished.

(b)   *Et avrare debet p<er> una<m> dieta<m> et quiet<us> es<t> de ij op<er>ib<us>*

And he must perform carrying service for one day's journey and he is quit of two dayworks.

(c) *Et si equu<m> vendid<er>it inf<ra> man<er>iu<m> v<e>l ext<ra> ex<cepti>s Nundinis dabit ad theolon<ium> ijd.*

And if he shall have sold a horse within the manor or outside, except at time of fairs, he shall pay toll 2d.

(d) *Ide<m> d<ebet> met<er>e in autu<m>pno v<idelicet> uno die cu<m> uno ho<m>i<n>e s<e>c<un>do die cu<m> duob<us> ho<m>i<n>ib<us> s<i>n<e> cibo*

The same must reap in autumn namely one day with one man a second day with two men without food.

(e) *... t<ert>io die duos ho<m>i<n>es ad magnu<m> metebene et erit custos eo<rum> tota die*

... on the third day two men at the great boon-reaping and he will be responsible for their food all day.

(f) *Ide<m> d<ebet> arare bis in yeme et semel in quadrages<ima>*

The same must plough twice in winter and once in Lent.

(g) *It equ<um> no<n> deb<et> vende<re> s<i>n<e> lic<encia> d<omi>ni*

Likewise he must not sell a horse without the lord's permission.

(h) *Ide<m> deb<et> merchet pro filia sua maritanda ad vol<untatem> d<omi>ni*

The same owes merchet for marrying off his daughter, at the will of the lord.

Example 30 (p. 67)

Joh<anne>s le bonde ten<et> j virg<atam> t<er>re p<ro> qua solvit annuatim ijs. ad t<er>min<os> s<an>c<t>i m<ar>tini et s<an>c<t>i Joh<ann>is
Ide<m> inve<n>iet unu<m> ho<m>i<n>em ad levand<um> fenu<m> uno t<oto> (?) die s<i>n<e> cibo q<ua>cumq<ue> d<omi>n<u>s volu<er>it et cariabit duas carectatas fen<i> ad orreu<m> d<omi>ni de Burton' vid<elicet> qu<ando> fit cariagium de sydhaluh (?) Qu<ando> no<n> fit cariagiu<m> de Foredeles usq<ue> Bronston si<mi>l<ite>r cariabit duas carect<as> ibid et q<ua>n<do> ap<u>d Burton' tres carectatas Ide<m> d<ebet> sarcl<i>are uno die t<otu>m (?) cu<m> uno ho<m>i<n>e c<on>tra fest<um> nat<ivitatis> s<an>c<t>i Joh<anni>s bapt<iste> similit<er> s<i>n<e> cibo Id d<ebet> met<er>e in autu<m>pno v<idelicet> uno die cu<m> uno ho<m>i<n>e s<e>c<un>do die cu<m> duob<us> ho<m>i<ni>b<us> s<i>n<e> cibo Et t<er>cio die inve<n>iet duos ho<m>i<n>es ad magnu<m> metebene et erit custos eo<rum> tota die stans cu<m> v<er>ga (?) et respondebit d<omi>no p<ro> custodia sua si male agat<ur> et h<ab>ebunt bini et bini dous panes unu<m> de fr<ument>o et aliu<m> de silig<o>

John le Bond holds one virgate of land for which he pays annually 2s. at the terms of Saint Martin and Saint John.
The same shall find one man for lifting hay for one whole day without food wheresoever the lord shall have wished and he shall carry two cartloads of hay to the barn of the lord of Burton, namely when he does carriage service of shingles (?). When he does not do carriage service of faredels (?) to Branston similarly he shall carry two cartloads there and when to Burton three cartloads.

The same must hoe for one day with one man before the feast of the nativity of Saint John the Baptist similarly without food. The same must reap in autumn, namely for one day with one man, for a second day with two men without food. And on the third day he shall find two men for the great boon-reaping and he shall be responsible for them for the whole day, remaining in charge, and he shall answer to the lord for his care if it (i.e. the work) is badly done, and they shall have two loaves apiece, one of wheat and the other of rye.

Example 31 (p. 69)

Will<elmu>s cok tenet una<m> virgatam t<er>re cu<m> p<er>tinentiis et qu<ando> plene op<er>at<ur> solvit p<er> annu<m> x denar<ios> ad festu<m> s<an>c<t>i michael<is> Et q<ua>libet septimana op<er>abili a p<re>d<i>c<t>o festo usq<ue> ad festu<m> s<an>c<t>i Pet<ri> ad vinc<u>la debet op<er>ari p<er> t<res> dies q<ua>l<e>cu<n>q<ue> op<us> d<omi>n<u>s voluerit Et qu<ando> t<ri>turat debet t<ri>turare de quolibet blado j estrich<am> n<isi> de avena de q<ua> t<ri>turabit dimid<ium> q<uar>t<erium> Et quotiens aliud op<us> facit op<er>abitur usq<ue> ad hora<m> t<er>tiam et hoc facere debet sine stipendio It et p<er> un<u>m die<m> in yeme vel in xl<a> qu<ando> sum<m>onit<us> fu<er>it s<e>c<un>d<u>m q<uo>d h<abe>t ad caruca<m> arare debet una<m> ac<ra>m Et sing<u>lis annis in vig<i>l<ia> s<an>c<t>i martini duc<er>e debet caru̇cam suam ad locu<m> ubi caruce d<omi>ni arant et ibi arare debet ac<ra>m et dimid<iam> et a g<ra>nario d<omi>ni portare debet sem<e>n ad locu<m> p<re>dictu<m> et seminare p<re>d<ic>tam t<er>ra<m> et herciare et ob hoc debet es<se> quiet<us> de t<ri>b<us> op<er>ib<us> It cont<ra> Natale et Pascha parare debet dimid<ium> q<ua>rt<erium> brasii et cu<m> faragine d<omi>ni siccare et ad molendinu<m> d<omi>ni cariare et ibi s<er>vienti d<omi>ni lib<er>are Et si ad vicinu<m> molendinu<m> molari debet tu<n>c lib<er>abit illud in curia d<omi>ni et ob hoc quiet<us> es<se> debet de j op<er>e It de om<n>ib<us> porcis s<ibi> nutritis v<e>l emptis pannagiu<m> dare debet ad Natale scil<icet> de quolib<et> porco sup<er>annuato j denar<ium> Et de porco dimid<ij> anni ob<olum> Debet eciam de herbagio ad eund t<er>minu<m> p<ro> quolibet grosso averio duo<rum> anno<rum> et dimid<ij> ijd. et ad festu<m> s<an>c<t>i Joh<ann>is bapt<ist>e jd. et p<ro> quolibet duo<rum> anno<rum> jd. ad Natale et ad festu<m> s<an>c<t>i Joh<ann>is bapt<ist>e ob<olum> It debe<t> in xl<a> h<er>ciare p<er> j die<m> usq<ue> ad hora<m> nona<m> cu<m> j equo sine cibo It debet oves lavare et tondere cu<m> ij hominib<us> et ip<s>e int<er>es<se> si d<omi>n<u>s voluerit et vid<er>e q<uo>d b<e>n<e> faciant et p<er> t<re>s dies integ<ro>s sarclare et semel h<abe>re correediu<m>

William Cok holds a virgate of land with appurtenances and when he works fully he pays annually 10d. at the feast of Saint Michael and in any week of works from the aforesaid feast until the feast of Saint Peter in Chains he must work for three days at whatever work the lord shall have wished. And when he threshes he must thresh of whatever [sort of] corn one strike unless [it is] of oats of which he shall thresh a half quarter. And as often as he performs other work he shall work until the third hour and this he must do without payment. And also he must plough one acre according to whatever he has for ploughing for one day in winter or in Lent when he shall have been summoned. And every year on the eve of Saint Martin he must take his plough to the place where the lord's ploughs are ploughing and there he must plough an acre and a half and he must carry seed from the lord's granary to the aforesaid place and sow the aforesaid land and harrow [it] and for this he must be quit of three dayworks. Also in preparation for Christmas and Easter he must prepare half a quarter of malt and dry it with the lord's straw and carry it to the lord's mill and there deliver it to the lord's servant. And if he must grind at a neighbouring mill then he shall deliver it to the lord's courtyard and for this he must be quit of one daywork. Also of all pigs weaned for himself or bought he must give pannage at Christmas, namely for each pig of one to two years old 1d. and for a pig of half a year old a halfpenny. Furthermore for pasturage he must pay at the same term for each draught animal of two and a half years 2d. and at the feast of Saint John the Baptist 1d. and for each [draught animal] of two years 1d. at Christmas and at the feast of Saint John the Baptist a halfpenny. Also he must harrow in Lent for one day until the ninth hour with one horse without food. Also he must wash and shear sheep with two men and be present himself if the lord shall have wished and see that they work well and hoe for three whole days and have a food allowance once.

Select Dictionary

Only spellings used in this book are included. For variant spelling consult the recommended medieval Latin dictionary. Nouns are shown in the nominative case with genitive ending and gender indicated; verbs are shown with the usual principal parts, for example, first person present tense, infinitive, perfect and supine stems; adjectives are shown with gender endings indicated; prepositions are followed by an indication of the case they take.

abl.	ablative		gen.	genitive
acc.	accusative		imp.	impersonal
adj.	adjective		m.	masculine
conj.	conjugation		n.	neuter
dat.	dative		pl.	plural
dep.	deponent		prep.	preposition
f.	feminine		pres. part.	present participle

The letters 'c' and 't' are often indistinguishable in medieval hands and are used variably; in this book 't' is preferred to 'c' if there is doubt; the letters 'i' and 'j' are treated as the same letter.

a, ab (prep and abl.) from, by
abbas, -atis (m.) abbot
abbathia, -ie (f.) abbey
abbutto, -are, -avi, -atum to abut, adjoin
abiuro, -are, -avi, -atum to renounce
ac (conj.) and
accido, -ere, accidi to fall due
accio, -ionis (f.) (legal) action
acra, -e (f.) acre
ad (prep and acc.) to, at, for
adiaceo, -ere, -ui, -itum to adjoin
adjudico, -are, -avi, -atum to adjudge
admitto, -ere, -misi, -missum to admit
   petivit admitti tenens he petitioned to be
   admitted tenant
afferator, -oris (m.) assessor, affeerer
affirmo, -are, -avi, -atum to affirm
affraia, -e (f.) affray
ago, -ere, egi, actum to do
aliquis, aliquid (pron.) anyone, anything
aliquo modo in any way
alius, -a, -ud (pron. and adj.) other, another
alterus, -a, -um (adj.) other
ex altera parte on the other side
ambo (adv.) both
amerciamentum, -i (n.) amercement, fine
Anglia, -e (f.) England
Anglice (adv.) in English
animal, -e (n.) animal

annuatim (adv.) annually
annus, -i (m.) year
ante (prep and acc.) before
ab antiquo tempore from ancient times
antiquus, -a, -um (adj.) ancient
aperio, -ire, -ui, -tum to open up
apparentia, -ie (f.) appearance (in court)
apud (prep and acc) at, near
aqua, -e (f.) water
arabilis, -e (adj.) arable
aratrum, -i (n.) plough
armiger, -eri (m.) esquire
arreragium, -i (n.) arrears, usually pl.
arro, -are, -avi, -atum to plough
also *aro*
articulus, -i (m.) article, clause
assignatus, -i (m.) assign, assignee
assisa, -e (f.) assize
   fregerunt assisam panis et cervisie they broke
   the assize of bread and ale
attachio, -iare, -iavi, -iatum to attach
attornamentum, -i (n.) attornment,
   acknowledgment
attornatus, -i (m.) attorney
attorno, -are, -avi, -atum to acknowledge
auca, -e (f.) goose
autumpnus, -i (m.) autumn
avena, -e (f.) oats
averium, -ii (n.) beast, draught animal

averagium, -ii (n.) carriage service
avraro, -are, -avi, -atum to perform carrying
    service
avus, -i (m.) grandfather

ballivius, -ii (m.) bailiff
baro, -onis (m.) tenant-in-chief, baron
    curia baronis court baron
beatus, -a, -um (adj.) blessed
bene (adv.) well, truly
bidens, -entis (f.) sheep
bigarius, -ii (m.) carter
bini et bini (adv.) two and two
bis (adv.) twice
bladum, -i (n.) corn, cornfield
borialis, -e (adj.) northern
    borialiter (adv.) on the north
bos, bovis, -e (m.) ox
bosca, -e (f.) wood, firewood
    also *boscum*
boteler (m.) butler
bovata, -e (f.) bovate
bracio, -are, -avi, -atum to brew
    also *brasio*
brasiator, -oris (m., f.) brewer
brasium, -ii (m.) malt
bruaria, -e (f.) heath
burgagium, -ii (n.) burgage

calumpnio, -iare, -iavi, -iatum to challenge,
    charge
campus, -i (m.) field
canis, -is (m.) dog
cantaria, -e (f.) chantry
capellanus, -i (m.) chaplain
capio, -ere, cepi, captum to take
capitalis, -e (adj.) chief
caput, -is (n.) head
    prout patet in capite as appears above his
    name
carcer, -eris (m.) prison
carectata, -e (f.) cartload also *carecta, -e* (f.)
cariagium, -ii (n.) carriage
cario, -are, -avi, -atum to carry
caro, carnis (f.) flesh, meat
carpentarius, -ii (m.) carpenter
caruca, -e (f.) plough
cementarius, -i (m.) mason
certus, -a, -um certain
cervisia, -e (f.) ale
    also *servisia*
(de) cetero in the future
cibum, -i (n.) food

ciminium, -ii (n.) cummin
circa (adv.,prep. and acc.) around
cirotecarius, -ii (m.) glover
citra (adv., prep. and acc.) since
clameum, -ei (n.) claim
clarus, -a, -um (adj.) net
claudo, -ere, clausi, clausum to close
    diem clausit extremum he died
clausura, -e (f.) close also *clausum, -i* (n.)
clericus, -i (m.) clerk
cognosco, -ere, -gnovi, cognitum to
    acknowledge
cohabito, -are, -avi, -atum to live with
collector, -oris (m.) collector
columbare, -is (n.) or *columbarium, -i* (n.)
    dovecot
communis, -e (adj.) common
    de communi secta of common suit of court
communiter (adv.) commonly
compareo, -ere, parui to appear (in court)
compotus, -i (m.) account
concedo, -ere, -cessi, -cessum to grant
concelamentum, -i (n.) concealment
concordor, -ari, -atus sum (dep.) to come to
    terms, agree with;
    pro licencia concordanda for licence to
    agree
concubina, -e (f.) concubine
confessor, -oris (m.) confessor
cohabito, -are, -avi, -atum to dwell together
conlibet it pleases, it is agreeable
conquerens, -entis (m., f.) plaintiff
Conquestus, -us (m.) (Norman) Conquest
considero, -are, -avi, -atum to give judgement
consuetudo, -inis (f.) custom
    secundum consuetudinem manerii according
    to the custom of the manor
consuetus, -a, -um, to be accustomed
contra (adv., prep. and acc.) before, against,
    in preparation for
copia, -e (f.) copy
    per copiam by copy [of court roll]
coram (adv., prep. and abl.) before
corredium, -ii (n.) food allowance
cotagium, -ii (n.) cottage
crastinum, -i (n.) morrow
    in crastino on the morrow
crux, crucis (f.) cross
crofta, -e (f.) croft
culpabilis, -e (adj.) guilty
cum (conj., prep. and abl.) with
cunstabularius, -i (m.) constable
curia, -e (f.) court, courtyard

curia baronis court baron; *curia customaria*
customary court; *curia leta* court leet;
   curia magna great court; *curia parva* small
court; *curia prima* first court
curtilagium, -ii (n.) curtilage, yard
custumarius, -a, -um (adj.) customary also
   customarius, -a, -um
   customarius tenens customary tenant
custodia, -e (f.) custody, care
custos, -odis (m.) keeper, person responsible

dampnum, -i (n.) damages
debeo, -ere, -ui, -itum to owe, to be obliged [to
   do something]
debitum, -i (n.) debt
decennaria, -e (f.) tithing
decennarius, -ii (m.) tithingman
decessus, -us (m.) death
decima, -e (f.) tithe
decimus nonus nineteenth
decollatio, -onis (f.) beheading
decurro, -currere, -cucurri, -cursum to run down
   [water]
defalta, -e (f.) default
defectus, -us (m.) default
defendens, -entis (m. and f.) defendant
deficio, -ere, -feci, -fectum to default
defunctus, -a, -um (adj.) deceased
denarius, -ii (m.) penny
depono, -ere, -posui, -positum to lay down [i.e.
   a surface]
destruo, -ere, -struxi, -structum to destroy
detineo, -ere, -ui, -itum to detain, keep back
Deus, -i (m.) God
devido, -ere, -visi, -visum to divide
dico, -ere, -dixi, dictum to say
dictus, -a, -um (the) said
dies, diei (m.) day; (f.) when meaning is
   'appointed day'
   dies dominica Sunday, *dies Lune* Monday,
   dies Martis Tuesday, *dies Mercurii*
   Wednesday, *dies Jovis* Thursday, *dies
   Veneris* Friday, *dies Sabbati* Saturday
dieta, -e (f.) day's journey
dimidius, -a, -um (adj.) half
dimitto, -ere, -misi, -missum to lease, demise
dispersim (adv.) here and there, dispersedly
districtio, -ionis (f.) distraint
distringo, -ere, -inxi, -ictum to distrain
diutius (adv.) longer
diversus, -a, -um (adj.) various
divisio, -ionis (f.) piece of land
do, dare, dedi, datum to give
dola, -e (f.) dole, (share)

domina, -e (f.) lady
Dominica, -e (f.) Sunday
dominicalis, -e (adj.) demesne
dominium, -i (n.) demesne land
dominus, -i (m.) lord, Sir
domus, -us (f.) house
donum, -i (n.) gift
dos, dotis (f.) dowry
duco, -ere, duxi, ductum to lead
   ducens leading
duo, duarum (pl. only) two
duodecimus, -a, -um twelfth
   duodecimi the 12 [jurors]
duro, -are, -avi, -atum to last, extend
   durante minore etate during [their]
   minority

ecclesia, -e (f.) church
   ecclesie Anglicane/Hibernice of the
   English/Irish church
ecclesiasticus, -a, -um (adj.) ecclesiastical,
   church
edificium, -ii (n.) building
effodio, -ire, -fodi, -fossum to dig
elapsus, -a, -um (adj.) elapsed, past
eleccio, -ionis (f.) choice
eligo, -ere, -legi, -lectum to elect
emendo, -are, -avi, -atum to repair
emo, emere, emi, emptum to buy
episcopus, -i (m.) bishop
equus, -i (m.) horse
eschaeta, -e (f.) escheat
essonia, -e (f.) essoin
essonio, -are, -avi, -atum to essoin
estas, -atis (f.) summer
estimatio, -onis (f.) estimation
estricha, -e (f.) strike [dry measure]
etas, -atis (f.) age
ex (prep. and acc.) out of, from
excipio, -ere, -cepi, -ceptum to except
excessivus, -a, -um (adj.) excessive
excludo, -ere, -clusi, clusum to exclude
exeo, -ire, -ivi, -itum to issue from
exigo, -ere, exegi, exactum to demand
existo, -ere, -stiti, -stitum to be, exist
   iacens et existens in lying and being in
exitus, -us (m.) issues, revenue, profits,
   offspring
extenta, -e (f.) extent, survey
extra (adv., prep. and acc.) outside
extraho, -trahere, -traxi, -tractum to draw out
extraneus, -a, -um (adj.) foreign
ewangelista, -e (m.) evangelist

facio, -ere, feci, factum to make, do

falcatio, -ionis (f.) mowing
falco, -are, -avi, -atum to mow
falda, -e (f.) foldyard
familia, -e (f.) household
faragina, -e (f.) straw
fensura, -e (f.) fence
fenum, -i (n.) hay
feodum, -i (n.) fee
festum, -i (m.) feast, festival
fidelitas, -atis (f.) fealty
fideliter (adv.) faithfully
fides, fidei (f.) faith
   fidei defensoris [of the] defender of the
   faith
filia, -e (f.) daughter
filius, -ii (m.) son
finis, -is (m.) fine
   fecit finem pro ingressu he paid an entry
   fine
firma, -e (f.) rent, fixed payment
firmarius, -ii (m.) farmer, renter
foragium, -ii (n.) fodder
fore (used as future infinitive of *sum*)
forisfactum, -i (n.) [also *forisfactura, -e* (f.)]
   penalty, forfeiture
forma, -e (f.) form, terms
fossatum, -i (n.) ditch
Francia, -e (f.) France
franciplegius, -ii (m.) frankpledge,
   tithingman
frango, -ere, fregi, fractum to break
frater, fratris (m.) brother
frumentum, -i (n.) wheat
furma see *firma*
furnacium -i (n.) furnace, oven, kiln house
futurus, -a, -um (future participle of *sum*)

gallina, -e (f.) hen
gardinum, -i (n.) garden
generosus, -i (m.) gentleman
gersumo, -are, -avi, -atum to pay a fine
glandia, -arum (f. and pl.) acorns
granarium, -ii (n.) granary
grangiarius, -ii (m.) granger
gratia, -e (f.) favour, grace
grossus, -a, -um (adj.) large
guilda, -e (f.) gild

habeo, -ere, -ui, -itum to have
   habendum et tenedum to have and to hold
   (+ dat.)
hamsocnan housebreak
hebdomeda, -e (f.) week
herbagium, -ii (n.) pasture

hercio, -are, -avi, -atum to harrow
hereditarius, -a, -um hereditary
hereditatio, -ionis (f.) inheritance
hereditizo, -are, -avi, -atum to inherit
heres, -edis (m. and f.) heir
herriettum, -i (n.) heriot
Hibernia, -e (f.) Ireland
hic, hec, hoc (pron. and adj.) this
hiems, hiemis (f.) winter also *yems*
homagium, -ii (n.) homage
homo, -inis (m.) man
honor, -oris (m.) honour (large feudal
   estate)
hora, -e (f.) hour
horreum, -ei (n.) barn
hospitium, -ii (n.) lodging house
humitorium, -i (n.) tanning yard
hutesium, -ii (n.) hue and cry
   levavit hutesium iuste he raised the hue
   and cry justly

iaceo, -ere, -ui, -itum to lie
ibidem (adv.) there, in the same place
idem, eadem, idem (pron.) the same
ideo (adv.) therefore
ignotus, -a, -um (adj.) unknown
imperpetuum (adv.) for ever, in perpetuity
imprimis (adv.) first
inde (adv.) thence
indentura, -e (f.) indenture
infra (adv.) within
ingressus, -us (m.) entry
iniuste (adv.) unjustly
inquisitio, -ionis (f.) inquiry
insalubris, -e (adj.) unhealthy
insuper (adv.) moreover
integer, -ra, -rum (adj.) whole
inter (adv., prep. and acc.) between
interficio, -ere, -feci, -fectum to kill
intersum, -esse, -fui to be present at
invenio, -ire, -veni, ventum to find
inventio, -ionis (f.) finding
   inventio sancte crucis the finding of the
   holy cross
ipse, ipsa, ipsum (pron. and adj.) self,
   he/she, himself/herself
is, ea, id (pron.) he, she, it
iste, ista, istud (pron. and adj.) he, she, it
item (adv.) likewise, also
iurator, -oris (m.) juror
iuro, -are, -avi, -atum to swear
   de iure by right
ius, iuris (n.) right

iuste (adv.) justly
iuxta (adv., prep and acc.) near, according
    to

lavo, -are, -avi, -atum to wash
ledo, -ere, lesi, lesum to injure
legitime (adv.) lawfully
legius, -i (m.) liege man
lerwite fine for unchastity
leta, -e (f.) leet
levo, -are, -avi, -atum to raise
    ad levandum fenum for making hay
lex, legis (f.) law
liber, -a, -um free
liberatio, -ionis (f.) allowance, delivery,
    handing over
libere (adv.) freely
libero, -are, -avi, -atum to deliver, hand over
libra, -e (f.) pound
licencia, -e (f.) permission
    pro licencia habenda for having permission
ligo, -are, -avi, -atum to tie up
locus, -i (m.) place

magister, -tri (m.) master
magnus, -a, -um (adj.) great
male (adv.) badly
mandra, -e (f.) hovel, cattle-pen
manerium, -ii (n.) manor
manupastus, -i (m.) household, member of
    household
manus, -us (f.) hand
    in manu[s] domini into the hand[s] of the
    lord
    sexto manu six-handed
marcella, -e (f.) mark
marito, -are, -avi, -atum to marry
medietas, -atis (f.) moiety, half
melius (adv.) better
merchetum, -i (n.) merchet
messor, -oris (m.) hayward
metebene, -is (n.) boon reaping
meto, -ere, messui, messum to reap
messuagium, -ii (n.) messuage
miles, -itis (m.) knight
minor, minus (adj.) smaller
    durante minore etate during [his] minority
misericordia, -e (f.) mercy, amercement
mitto, -ere, misi, missum to send
modo (adv.) now
molendinum, -i (n.) mill
molo, -are, -avi, -atum to grind
mordeo, -ere, momordi, morsum to bite
mors, mortis (f.) death

mortuus, -a, -um (adj.) dead
moveo, -ere, movi, motum to institute [a plea],
    move
multo, -onis (m.) sheep, wether

natale, -is (n.) birthday
nativitas, -atis (f.) birth
nativus, -i (m.) villein
necessarius, -a, -um (adj.) needful
necnon and also
nihil (indeclinable) or *nichil* nothing
nomen, -inis (n.) name
nomine (and gen.) in the name of
nonus, -a, -um ninth
noster, -ra, -rum (adj.) our
notitia, -e (f.) knowledge
nullus, -a, -um (adj.) no, not any
nunc (adv.) now
nundine, -arum (f. and pl.) fair
nuper (adv.) recently, lately
nutritus, -a, -um (adj.) weaned

ob (prep. and acc.) on account of
obeo, -ire, -ivi, -itum to go to meet
    obivavit he went to meet (unusual form)
obitus, -us (m.) death
obolus, -i (m.) halfpenny
    panis obolatus halfpenny loaf
obscuro, -are, -avi, -atum to scour
    quia non obscuravit fossata sua because he
    did not scour his ditches
obstupo, -are, -avi, -atum to obstruct
occido, -ere, -cidi, -cisum to kill
occupatio, -ionis (f.) occupation
octavus, -a, -um eighth
October, -bris (m.) October
offero, -erre, optuli (obtuli), oblatum to offer
    optulit se he appeared
officiarius, -ii (m.) officer, official
officium, -ii (n.) office
olim (adv.) formerly
omnino (adv.) entirely
omnis, -e (adj.) all
    omnia bene all is well
    omnia et singula all and singular
onero, -are, -avi, -atum to charge, make
    answerable for
onus, -eris (n.) charge [in accounts]
operabilis, -e (adj.) working
operatio, -ionis (f.) daywork
opero, -are, -avi, -atum to work
optimus, -a, -um (adj.) best
opus, operis (n.) work, use
    ad opus et usum to the use and behoof
ordino, -are, -avi, -atum to order

ovis, -is (f.) sheep

panis, -is (m.) bread, loaf

pannagium, -ii (n.) pannage also *pasnagium*

papa, -e (m.) pope

parcella, -e (f.) parcel, part

parcus, -i (m.) park

paro, -are, -avi, -atum to prepare

pars, -tis (f.) part
    ex una parte on one side

parvus, -a, -um (adj.) small

Pascha, -e (f.) Easter

pascua, -e (f.) grazing land, pasture

pastura, -e (f.) pasture

pater, -ris (m.) father

pateo, -ere, patuit to be manifest, appear
    prout patet as appears

pauper, -eris (adj.) poor

pax, pacis (f.) peace

pecia, -e (f.) piece

pena, -e (f.) penalty

per (prep. and acc.) by

percutio, -ere, -cussi, -cussum to strike

permitto, -ere, -misi, -missum to permit

pertica, -e (f.) perch [measure]

pertinentia, -e (f.) appurtenance

perquisitum, -i (n.) profit

peto, -ere, petivi, petitum to claim, petition
    petit legem he seeks judgement

pistor, -oris (m.) baker

placea, -e (f.) plot

placitum, -i (n.) plea
    de placito debiti in a plea of debt
    de placito defamationis in a plea of slander
    de placito dotis in a plea of dowry
    de placito transgressionis in a plea of trespass

plegius, -i (m.) pledge, surety

plene (adv.) fully

plenus, -a, -um (adj.) full
    in plena curia in open court

pomarium, -ii (n.) orchard

pono, -ere, posui, positum to produce [in court], place

ponit se he submits to [judgement]

porcus, -i (m.) pig

porto, -are, -avi, -atum to carry

possum, posse, potui to be able

post (adv., prep and acc.) after

posta, -e (f.) post

pratum, -i (n.) meadow

prebenda, -e (f.) prebend

precaria, -e (f.) boon work

preceptum est it is ordered (+ dat.)

predictus, -a, -um (adj.) aforesaid

prefatus, -a, -um (adj.) aforesaid

prejudicium, -i (n.) prejudice

premissa, -orum (n. and pl.) premises

premunio, -ire, -ivi, -itum to summon, warn

prepositus, -i (m.) reeve

presbyter, -eri (m.) priest

presentatio, -ionis (f.) presentment

presentia, -e (f.) presence

presento, -are, -avi, -atum to present, make presentment

pretendo, -ere, -i, -tentum to claim, allege

presto, -are, -avi, -atum to lend

preter (adv. & prep. and acc.) besides

pretium, -ii (n.) price
    also *precium*

primus, -a, -um (adj.) first

prioris, -is (m.) prior

prius (n. acc. of *prior* as adv.) formerly

pro (prep. and abl.) for

proclamatio, -ionis (f.) proclamation

procreo, -are, -avi, -atum to beget

proprius, -a, -um (adj.) own
    in propria persona sua in his own person

prosequor, -sequi, -secutus sum (dep.) to prosecute

prout (adv.) as

proximus, -a, -um (adj.) next

pulla, -e (f.) chicken

pullus, -i (m.) foal

Purificatio, -ionis (f.) purification

puteus, -i (m.) well
    puteis corariis (abl. and pl.) tanning vats

puto, -are, -avi, -atum to believe, think

pyncker[arius], -i butler, also *pincernarius*

Quadragesima, -e (f.) Lent

qualiscumque, qualecumque (adj.) whatever kind

qualitercumque (adv.) in whatsoever way

quando (adv. and conj.) when

quandocumque (adv.) whensoever

quare (adv.) wherefore

quarta, -e (f.) farthing

quarterium, -ii (n.) quarter (measure)

quattuor four.

-que [addition to end of word] and

querela, -e (f.) suit, action

querens, -entis (m. and f.) plaintiff

quero, -ere, quesivi, quesitum to seek

queror, queri, questus sum (dep.) to bring an action, complain

qui, que, quod (pron.) who, which, what
quia (conj.) because
quidam, quedam, quoddam (pron.) a certain
quidem indeed
    qui quidem who
quieteclamo, -are, -avi, -atum to quitclaim
quietus, -a, -um quit, free
quilibet, quelibet, quodlibet (pron.) each, any
    whatsoever
quintus, -a, -um fifth
quod (conj.) that
quondam (adv.) formerly
quoquomodo (adv.) in whatever place
quotiens (adv.) as often as
quousque (adv.) until

recepta, -e (f.) receipt, money received
recipio, -ere, -cepi, -ceptum to receive
rectus, -a, -um (adj.) right, direct (of heirs)
recupero, -are, -avi, -atum to recover
redditus, -us (m.) rent
reddo, -ere, -didi, -itum to render, pay
regina, -e (f.) queen
regnum, -i (n.) reign
relaxo, -are, -avi, -atum to release, remit
relevium, -ii (n.) relief (payment)
remaneo, -ere, remansi to remain
remitto, -ere, -misi, -missum to remise
renovo, -are, -avi, -atum to renew
reparatio, -ionis (f.) repairs, reparations
reparo, -are, -avi, -atum to repair
respectus, -us (m.) respite, adjournment
    in respectu ad proximam [curiam]
    adjourned to the next [court]
respondeo, -ere, -spondi, -sponsum to reply
revertio, -ionis (f.) reversion
rex, regis (m.) king
roda, -e (f.) rood (measure of land)
rubeus, -a, -um red
ruptura, -e (f.) gap, break [in fence]

Sabbati dies Saturday
sacer, -ra, -rum (adj.) sacred
sacramentum, -i (n.) oath
salvus, -a, -um (adj.) excepting only, saving
sanctus, -a, -um (adj.) holy, saint
sanguis, -inis (m.) blood
sanitas, -atis (f.) health
sarclo, -are, -avi, -atum to hoe also *sarclio*
saysio, -iare, -iavi, -atum to seize, take; also
    seisio
scilicet (adv.) namely

scio, scire, scivi, scitum to know
scituatus, -a, -um situated
scitus, -us (m.) site
Scotia, -e (f.) Scotland
se (refl. pron.) himself
seco, -are, -ui, sectum to cut
secta, -e (f.) suit [of court]
    de communi secta of common suit [of
    court]
secundum (adv., prep. and acc.) according
    to
seisina, -e (f.) possession
seisio, -iare, -iavi, -iatum to take possession of
    seisitus, -a, -um (adj.) seized
semel (adv.) once
semen, -inis (n.) seed
semino, -are, -avi, -atum to sow
semita, -e (f.) lane
senescallus, -i (m.) steward
senior, -ioris (adj.) senior
sepes, -is (f.) fence
septimana, -e (f.) week
sequens, -entis (pres. part.) following
servicium, -ii (n.) service
serviens, servientis (m. and f.) servant
servisia, -e (f.) ale
sextus decimus sixteenth
sic (adv.) so
sicco, -are, -avi, -atum to dry
siligo, -inis (f.) rye
similiter (adv.) similarly
sirpus, -i (m.) rush
sive ... sive whether ... or
    sive plus sive minus more or less
soleo, -ere, solitus sum (semi-dep.) to be
    accustomed
solidus, -i (m.) shilling
solvo, -ere, solvi, solutum to pay
soror, -oris (f.) sister
specto, -are, -avi, -atum to belong to
stabula, -e (f.) stable
stans, -tis (pres. part.) standing
stipendium, -ii (n.) wages
sub (prep., abl. and acc.) under
summa, -e (f.) sum
    summa totalis sum of the total
summoneo, -ere, -ui, -itum to summon
sumptus, -us (m.) expense, charge
super (adv., prep. and acc.) above, on
superannuatus, -a, -um (adj.) one to two years
superius (adv.) previously, above
supervisus, -us (m.) survey

supradictus, -a, -um (adj.) above mentioned
supremus, -a, -um (adj.) supreme
    supremi capitis (gen.) supreme head
sursumredditio, -ionis (f.) surrender
sursumreddo, -ere, -reddidi, -reditum to
    surrender
suus, -a, -um (adj.) his, her, their

talis, -e (adj.) such
tallio, -iare, -iavi, -iatum to tax
tam ... quam both ... and
tango, tangere, tetigi, tactum to touch,
    concern
    de diversis articulis curiam tangentibus of
    the various articles touching the court
taurus, -i (m.) bull
tenementum, -i (n.) tenement
tenentiarius, -i (m.) tenant
tenens, -entis (m. and f.) tenant
teneo, -ere, tenui, tentum to hold
tenura, -e (f.) tenure
ter thrice
terminus, -i (m.) term
    eisdem terminis at the same terms
terra, -e (f.) land
tertius, -a, -um third
textor, -oris (m.) weaver
theologia, -e (f.) theology
theolonium, -i (n.) toll
tinctor, -oris (m.) dyer
titulus, -i (m.) title
tondeo, -ere, totondi, tonsum to shear
totus, -a, -um (adj.) all, the whole
traho, -ere, traxi, tractum to draw, haul
    traxit sanguinem he drew blood
transgressio, -ionis (f.) trespass
transgressor, -oris (m.) trespasser, offender
tres three
tricesimus, -a, -um thirtieth
Trinitas, -atis (f.) Trinity
trituro, -are, -avi, -atum to thresh
tunc (adv.) then

ubi (adv.) where
ubicumque (adv.) wheresoever
ullus, -a, -um (adj.) any
ulterius (adv.) furthermore
ultimus, -a, -um (adj.) last
ultra (adv., prep. and acc.) beyond
una cum together with
unde (adv.) whence
universus, -a, -um (adj.) the whole, all
unus, -a, -um (gen. *unius*) one

usque (adv.) up to, until
ut (adv. & conj.) in order that, as, that
uterque, utraque, utrumque (pron.) each
uxor, -is (f.) wife

vadio, -iare, -iavi, -iatum to give security for
    vadiavit ad legem he produced
    compurgators
vastum, -i (n.) waste [land]
vel (conj.) or
vendico, -are, -avi, -atum to claim
venditio, -ionis (f.) sale
vendo, -ire, vendidi, venditum to sell
venella, -e (f.) lane
venio, -ire, veni, ventum to come
verbero, -are, -avi, -atum to assault
veredictum, -i (n.) verdict
versus (adv., prep. and acc.) against, towards
verus, -a, -um (adj.) true
via, -e (f.) way, road
vicesimus, -a, -um twentieth
vicinus, -a, -um (adj.) neighbouring
vicinus, -i (m.) neighbouring
victualia (pl.) food
vicus, -i (m.) place
videlicet (adv.) namely
video, -ere, vidi, visum to see
vidua, -e (f.) widow
vigilia, -e (f.) eve, vigil
villa, -e (f.) vill, township
villanus, -i (m.) villein
vinculum, -i (n.) chain
    in festo sancti Petri in vincula on the feast
    of St Peter in chains
violentia, -e (f.) violence
virga, -e (f.) rod
per virgam by the rod
virgo, -inis (f.) virgin
virgata, -e (f.) virgate
vis, viris (f.) force
visus, -us (m.) view
visus franciplegii view of frankpledge
vita, -e (f.) life
vitulus, -i (m.) calf
vivens, -tis (pres. part) living
voco, -are, -avi, -atum to call
volo, velle, volui to wish, intend
voluntas, -atis (f.) wish, will

warantizo, -are, -avi, -atum to guarantee,
    warrant
westura, -e (f.) crop

yems (for *hiems, hiemis* (f.)) winter

Appendix A

Tables of Declensions, Adjectives and Conjugations

The following lists are intended to serve only for first, quick reference, and some of the forms rarely, if ever, encountered, in manorial records as for instance the vocative case of nouns, are omitted. For full tables of declensions and conjugations see Kennedy *op. cit.* or any good Latin grammar.

Example of First Declension Nouns
Terra (f.) 'land'

	(Singular)	(Plural)
(Nom.)	*terra*	*terse*
(Acc.)	*terram*	*terras*
(Gen.)	*terre*	*terrarum*
(Dat.)	*terre*	*terris*
(Abl.)	*terra*	*terris*

Examples of Second Declension Nouns
Dominus (m.) 'lord' *Ager* (m.) 'field' *Pratum* (n.) 'meadow'

(Singular)	(Plural)	(Singular)	(Plural)	(Singular)	(Plural)
dominus	*domini*	*ager*	*agri*	*pratum*	*prata*
dominum	*dominos*	*agrum*	*agros*	*pratum*	*prata*
domini	*dominorum*	*agri*	*agrorum*	*prati*	*pratorum*
domino	*dominis*	*agro*	*agris*	*prato*	*pratis*
domino	*dominis*	*agro*	*agris*	*prato*	*pratis*

Examples of Third Declension Nouns
Pater (m.) 'father' *Mater* (f.) 'mother' *Caput* (n.) 'head'

(Singular)	(Plural)	(Singular)	(Plural)	(Singular)	(Plural)
pater	*patres*	*mater*	*matres*	*caput*	*capita*
patrem	*patres*	*matrem*	*matres*	*caput*	*capita*
patris	*patrum*	*matris*	*matrum*	*capitis*	*capitum*
patri	*patribus*	*matri*	*matribus*	*capiti*	*capitibus*
patre	*patribus*	*matre*	*matribus*	*capite*	*capitibus*

Examples of Fourth Declension Nouns
Redditus (m.) 'rent' *Manus* (f.) 'hand'

(Singular)	(Plural)	(Singular)	(Plural)
redditus	*redditus*	*manus*	*manus*
redditum	*redditus*	*manum*	*manus*
redditus	*reddituum*	*manus*	*manuum*
redditui	*redditibus*	*manui*	*manibus*
redditu	*redditibus*	*manu*	*manibus*

Examples of Fifth Declension Nouns
Dies (m. sometimes f.) 'day' *res* (f.) 'thing'

(Singular)	(Plural)	(Singular)	(Plural)
dies	*dies*	*res*	*res*
diem	*dies*	*rem*	*res*
diei	*dierum*	*rei*	*rerum*
diei	*diebus*	*rei*	*rebus*
die	*diebus*	*re*	*rebus*

Examples of Adjectives Declining like First and Second Declension Nouns
Predictus, -a, -um 'aforesaid'

	(Singular)				(Plural)	
(m.)	(f.)	(n.)	(m.)	(f.)	(n.)
predictus	*predicta*	*predictum*	*predicti*	*predicte*	*predicta*
predictum	*predictam*	*predictum*	*predictos*	*predictas*	*predicta*
predicti	*predicte*	*predicti*	*predictorum*	*predictarum*	*predictorum*
predicto	*predicte*	*predicto*	*predictis*	*predictis*	*predictis*
predicto	*predicta*	*predicto*	*predictis*	*predictis*	*predictis*

Example of Declension of Selected Third Declension Adjective
Omnis 'all'

	(Singular)		(Plural)
(m. & f.)	(n.)	(m. & f.)	(n.)
omnis	*omne*	*omnes*	*omnia*
omnem	*omne*	*omnes*	*omnia*
omnis	*omnis*	*omnium*	*omnium*
omni	*omni*	*omnibus*	*omnibus*
omni	*omni*	*omnibus*	*omnibus*

Example of Declension of Present Participle
Iacens 'lying'

	(Singular)		(Plural)
(m. & f.)	(n.)	(m. & f.)	(n.)
iacens	*iacens*	*iacentes*	*iacentia*
iacentem	*iacens*	*iacentes*	*iacentia*
iacentis	*iacentis*	*iacentium*	*iacentium*
iacenti	*iacenti*	*iacentibus*	*iacentibus*
iacenti, -e	*iacenti, -e*	*iacentibus*	*iacentibus*

Example of Indefinite Pronoun
Quidam 'a certain person or thing'

	(Singular)			(Plural)	
(m.)	(f.)	(n.)	(m.)	(f.)	(n.)
quidam	*quedam*	*quoddam*	*quidam*	*quedam*	*quedam*
quemdam	*quamdam*	*quoddam*	*quosdam*	*quasdam*	*quedam*
cuiusdam	*cuiusdam*	*cuiusdam*	*quorumdam*	*quarumdam*	*quorumdam*
cuidam	*cuidam*	*cuidam*	*quibusdam*	*quibusdam*	*quibusdam*
quodam	*quadam*	*quodam*	*quibusdam*	*quibusdam*	*quibusdam*

Example of First Conjugation Verb
Voco, vocare, vocavi, vocatum 'to call, name'

INDICATIVE ACTIVE

Present	Future	Imperfect	Perfect
voco	*vocabo*	*vocabam*	*vocavi*
vocas	*vocabis*	*vocabas*	*vocavisti*
vocat	*vocabit*	*vocabat*	*vocavit*
vocamus	*vocabimus*	*vocabamus*	*vocavimus*
vocatis	*vocabitis*	*vocabatis*	*vocavistis*
vocant	*vocabunt*	*vocabant*	*vocaverunt*

Future Perfect	Pluperfect	PARTICIPLES	
vocavero	*vocaveram*	Present	*vocans*
vocaveris	*vocaveras*	Future	*vocaturus*
vocaverit	*vocaverat*		
vocaverimus	*vocaveramus*	Gerund	*vocandum*
vocaveritis	*vocaveratis*		
vocaverint	*vocaverant*		

SUBJUNCTIVE

Present	Imperfect
vocem	*vocarem*
voces	*vocares*
vocet	*vocaret*
vocemus	*vocaremus*
vocetis	*vocaretis*
vocent	*vocarent*

INDICATIVE PASSIVE

Present	Future	Imperfect	Perfect
vocor	*vocabor*	*vocabar*	*vocatus sum*
vocaris	*vocaberis<-re>*	*vocabaris<-re>*	*vocatus es*
vocatur	*vocabitur*	*vocabatur*	*vocatus est*
vocamur	*vocabimur*	*vocabamur*	*vocati sumus*
vocamini	*vocabimini*	*vocabamini*	*vocati estis*
vocantur	*vocabuntur*	*vocabantur*	*vocati sunt*

Present Infinitive: *vocare* Perfect Infinitive: *vocatus esse*
Perfect Participle: *vocatus* Gerundive: *vocandus*

Example of Second Conjugation Verb
teneo, tenere, tenui, tentum 'to hold'

INDICATIVE ACTIVE

Present	Future	Imperfect	Perfect
teneo	*tenebo*	*tenebam*	*tenui*
tenes	*tenebis*	*tenebas*	*tenuisti*
tenet	*tenebit*	*tenebat*	*tenuit*
tenemus	*tenebimus*	*tenebamus*	*tenuimus*
tenetis	*tenebitis*	*tenebatis*	*tenuistis*
tenent	*tenebunt*	*tenebant*	*tenuerunt*

Future Perfect	Pluperfect	PARTICIPLES	
tenuero	*tenueram*	Present	*tenens*
tenueris	*tenueras*	Future	*teniturus*
tenuerit	*tenuerat*		
tenuerimus	*tenueramus*	Gerund	*tenendum*
tenueritis	*tenueratis*		
tenuerint	*tenuerant*		

SUBJUNCTIVE

Present	Imperfect
teneam	*tenerem*
teneas	*teneres*
teneat	*teneret*
teneamus	*teneremus*
teneatis	*teneretis*
teneant	*tenerent*

INDICATIVE PASSIVE

Present	Future	Imperfect	Perfect
teneor	*tenebor*	*tenebar*	*tentus sum*
teneris	*teneberis<-re>*	*tenebaris<-re>*	*tentus es*
tenetur	*tenebitur*	*tenebatur*	*tentus est*
tenemur	*tenebimur*	*tenebamur*	*tenti sumus*
tenemini	*tenebimini*	*tenebamini*	*tenti estis*
tenentur	*tenebuntur*	*tenebantur*	*tenti sunt*

Present Infinitive: *tenere* Perfect Infinitive: *tentus esse*
Perfect Participle: *tentus* Gerundive: *tenendus*

Example of Third Conjugation Verb
Concedo 'to grant' *concedo, concedere, concessi, concessum*

INDICATIVE ACTIVE

Present	Future	Imperfect	Perfect
concedo	*concedam*	*concedebam*	*concessi*
concedis	*concedes*	*concedebas*	*concessisti*
concedit	*concedet*	*concedebat*	*concessit*
concedimus	*concedemus*	*concedebamus*	*concessimus*
condeditis	*concedetis*	*concedebatis*	*concessistis*
concedunt	*concedent*	*concedebant*	*concesserunt*

Future Perfect	Pluperfect	PARTICIPLES	
concessero	*concesseram*	Present	*concedens*
concesseris	*concesseras*	Future	*concediturus*
concesserit	*concesserat*		
concesserimus	*concesseramus*	Gerund	*concedendum*
concesseritis	*concesseratis*		
concesserint	*concesserant*		

SUBJUNCTIVE

Present	Imperfect
concedam	*concederem*
concedas	*concederes*
concedat	*concederet*
concedamus	*concederemus*
concedatis	*concederetis*
concedant	*concederent*

INDICATIVE PASSIVE

Present	Future	Imperfect	Perfect
concedor	*concedar*	*concedebar*	*concessus sum*
concederis<-re>	*concederis<-re>*	*concedebaris<-re>*	*concessus es*
conceditur	*concedetur*	*concedebatur*	*concessus est*
concedimur	*concedemur*	*concedebamur*	*oncessi sumus*
concedimini	*concedemini*	*concedebamini*	*concessi estis*
conceduntur	*concedentur*	*concedebantur*	*concessi sunt*

Present Infinitive: *concedere* Perfect Infinitive: *concessus esse*
Perfect Participle: *concessus* Gerundive: *concedendus*

Example of Fourth Conjugation Verb
audio, audire, audivi, auditum 'to hear'

INDICATIVE ACTIVE

Present	Future	Imperfect	Perfect
audio	*audiam*	*audiebam*	*audivi*
audis	*audies*	*audiebas*	*audivisti*
audit	*audiet*	*audiebat*	*audivit*
audimus	*audiemus*	*audiebamus*	*audivimus*
auditis	*audietis*	*audiebatis*	*audivistis*
audiunt	*audient*	*audiebant*	*audiverunt*

Future Perfect	Pluperfect	PARTICIPLES	
audivero	*audiveram*	Present	*audiens*
audiveris	*audiveras*	Future	*auditurus*
audiverit	*audiverat*		
audiverimus	*audiveramus*	Gerund	*audiendum*
audiveritis	*audiveratis*		
audiverint	*audiverant*		

SUBJUNCTIVE

Present	Imperfect
audiam	*audirem*
audias	*audires*
audiat	*audiret*
audiamus	*audiremus*
audiatis	*audiretis*
audiant	*audirent*

INDICATIVE PASSIVE

Present	Future	Imperfect	Perfect
audior	*audiar*	*audiebar*	*auditus sum*
audiris	*audieris<-re>*	*audiebaris<-re>*	*auditus es*
auditur	*audietur*	*audiebatur*	*auditus est*
audimur	*audiemur*	*audiebamur*	*auditi sumus*
audimini	*audiemini*	*audiebamini*	*auditi estis*
audiuntur	*audientur*	*audiebantur*	*auditi sunt*

Present Infinitive: *audire* Perfect Infinitive: *auditus esse*
Perfect Participle: *auditus* Gerundive: *audiendus*

A general Alphabet of the Old Law Hands.

Appendix C

Types of Abbreviation Mark Found in Manorial Records, with Examples.

All the following forms of abbreviation can be found in the documents reproduced in this book, and three of these documents are analysed in detail to illustrate abbreviation marks in different hands at different periods.

(1.) **General Marks of Suspension and Contraction**

a. The scribe may write only the first part of the word and indicates his suspension of other letters by a mark. This mark may take various forms, such as an extension of the last letter written, e. g.

         =   *Cur<ia>*   (Example 6, line 1)

         =   *b<e>n<e>*   (Example 15, line 13)

b. A terminal *'t'* frequently has the bar crossing it extended into a curl, for instance;

         =   *volunt<atem>*   (Example 13, line 8)

c. The abbreviation mark may be a simple horizontal stroke, straight or wavy, over, e.g.

         =   *seq<uentem>*   (Example 27, line 2)

d. The scribe may write only the first letter(s) and the last letter(s), indicating his contraction of the word by a line over, which may pass through the ascenders of the tall letters, e.g.

         =   *Joh<ann>es*   (Example 6, line 1)

e. Another general sign of abbreviation consists of a backward curve ending in a strong, pendent comma, e.g.

         =   *Armig<er>i*   (Example 9, line 1)

         =   *s<olidos>*   (Example 28, line 2 and numerous others)

f. A vertical looped mark was at first used as a general abbreviation sign but later was usually restricted to represent *-es* or *-is* especially as terminal letters, e.g.

         =   *Milit<is>*   (Example 14, line 11)

Scribes of manorial records, often writing under pressure, were prone to use these general signs loosely and hastily, and often developed their own distinctive style. Only practice in a particular hand can produce accurate transcriptions.

(2.) **Modification of letters to indicate abbreviation**

This is most commonly found for letter 'p', which can be modified in a number of ways.

a. A bar written through the descender as a separate stroke or starting from the bottom of the descender means p<er> or p<ar>, e.g.

     =   sup<er>   (Example 4(a), line 1)

b. When the bar through the descender starts from the top of the down stroke or from the loop of the 'p' and goes left before it curls back to cross the tail, it signifies p<ro> e.g.

     =   p<ro>ut   (Example 16, line 2)

c. A flourish above the 'p', like the general sign of abbreviation described above, or like a comma, means p<re>.

     =   p<re>sent<ant>   (Example 7, line 3)

     =   p<re>d<icto>   (Example 25, line 20)

d. The letter 'r' following 'a' or 'e', known as the 'Arabic-2 small r' came in time to be used mostly to signify the genitive plural ending -rum, e.g.

     =   porco<rum>   (Example 28, line 1)

(3.) **Abbreviation by superior letters**

a. A letter or letters written above the normal level of the line usually indicates the omission of two or more letters, of which the superior letter is one. Letter 'q' is frequently followed by such letters, e.g.

     =   q<ueritur>   (Example 11, line 6)

     =   q<ua>da<m>   (Example 18, line 4)

b. A superior 'a' with a short extension over the top of this letter, often signifies the omission of -ra, e.g.

     =   t<ra>xit   (Example 10, line 7)

     =   cont<ra>   (Example 11, line 7)

(4.) **Some abbreviation marks are significant in themselves, actually indicating which letters are missing**.

a.   A sign like an Arabic figure 9 on the line, with a descender, signifies *con-*; placed above the line it signifies *-us*, e.g.

           =   *<con>q<ue>rente<m>*   (Example 18, line 1)

b.   The sign that looks rather like a modern cursive 'z' or an Arabic figure 3 usually abbreviated three classes of words; those with a dative or ablative ending in *-bus* in which the sign stands for the last two letters *-us*; those ending in *-que* in which the sign stands for the *-ue*; and those words which end in *-et* in which the sign replaces the *-et* ; e.g.

         =   *finib<us>*   (Example 3(a))

         =   *usq<ue>*   (Example 27, line 2)

         =   *ten<et>*   (Example 30, line 1)

c.   A sign somewhat like a superscript printed 'z' is often found at the end of a third person singular verb in the passive voice, e.g.

         =*saysiat<ur>* (Example 18, line 5)

The following three examples are chosen for detailed examination because of the variety and number of their abbreviations, and how they were written at different periods.

Example 9.   A mid-16th century hand.

Line 1   Note the use of 〈ʾ〉 as a general sign of suspension in *armg<er>i* and on a number of other occasions in this document.
hered<is> (note the sign for the final *-is*).

Lines 2-3   The curl on the crossing of the 't' in *attornament<o>*, which indicates the omission, is hardly discernible. The scribe in this document often uses a carelessly made general sign of contraction, with the last letter extended to the right, as in *ib<ide>m*. But note also that a final flourish may be made unnecessarily, when the word has not been abbreviated, as in *Edwardi*.

Line 3   Note the graceful suspension mark in *gr<ati>a*.

Line 5   A good example of a mark which indicates which letters have been omitted is found in *capit<is>*.

Line 6   The scribe uses a quick upward stroke to indicate letters omitted after 'r' as in *iur<e>*. There are other examples of this in the document.
There appears to be no abbreviation mark to indicate omissions in *ux<or>is*.
A good example of the abbreviation for *p<er>* in which the descender is crossed by a stroke which starts from the loop and which might thus have been confused with *p<ro>*.

Line 9   The flourish at the end of *curiam* might have been mistaken for an abbreviation; there are three words contracted in this line – *Om<n>es, lib<er>e, q<ua>m;* four with examples of suspension – *nat<ivi>* with only a tiny curl on the final *'t'*, *ten<entes>* in which the the fact that letters are omitted is shown by a strong horizontal line, *firmar<ii>*, with the final long *'r'* is continued by an upward stroke (compare the word in line 6), and *exact<i>*, again with only a faint sign after the *'t'*, and the fifth word is a hastily formed ampersand.

Line 14   Compare the suspension mark of *p<re>fati* with the similar mark of abbreviation in line 1.

Example 18. (a). mid-13th century hand.

This is a very attractive hand, and is not nearly so difficult as it may at first seem. The document has examples of most of the abbreviation signs likely to be encountered in this early period. Line 1 has 11 words abbreviated in its total of 14.

Line 1   *Q<ue>rela:* the abbreviation is indicated by a superior letter.
              Int<er> the abbreviation mark is a general sign of suspension at the end of a word, as in 1(a) above.
              <con>q<ue>rente<m>: this word has three different abbreviation signs – the sign for *con-*, the superior letter and the horizontal stroke over.
              p<re>po<s>itu<m>: note the flourish above the first *'p'*, the horizontal line indicating suspension and another horizontal above the *'u'* which often signifies the omission of terminal *'m'*.
              defend<entem>: a bar through the curved ascender of the *'d'* is all that stands for the last five letters.
              r<espect>u: this has a horizontal extension of the *'r'* and a superior letter, and the word is extremely contracted.
              usq<ue>: here the *'q'* has been modified, as described in 4(b) above, by a mark attached to its descender.
              cur<ia>: has the graceful suspension mark of 1(f) above.
              p<ro>xi<ma>m: here are the modified *'p'* of 2(b) above, and a superior letter *'a'*.

Line 2   *et et<iam>*: did you think at first that the word *et* had been repeated, or did you notice the horizontal line above the second *et*?
              q<uia> note this example of abbreviation type 4(a).

Line 4   *Av<er>il*: the mark that looks like a poorly formed *'s'* above the *'u'* *'v'>* signifies the omission of *-er*.

Line 5   *saysiat<ur>*: an example of the special mark signifying omission of *-ur* in a passive voice verb.

Line 7   *scilic<et>*: here the sign like a cursive *'z'*, of type 4(b), is used to signify *-et*.

Example 25. This document illustrates abbreviations used in a rental of the mid-16th century written in a careful legal hand. It contains many, if not most, of the types of abbreviation listed above.

Line 1 Note the curl after the *'d'* to indicate omission of the final letters of *redd<itus>*. Similarly a little curl on the *'s'* of *mes<suagio>*.

A good example of the bar through the *'p'* which is a continuation of the loop of the *'p'* but coming from the right and from below, thus signifying *p<er>*; note curl of the *'n'* in *p<er>tinen<tiis>*.

The horizontal stroke indicating omission of letters in *ib<ide>m* goes through the ascender of the *'b'*; there is an apparently unnecessary flourish after the *'m'*.

Line 2 Another example of the horizontal stroke through the ascenders of *Will<elm>i*.

Line 3 Note the example of abbreviation type 1(b) in *exeunt<is>* and of 1(e) in *div<er>s<is>*; only a vertical stroke after the *'l'* to signify the final letters of *p<ar>cell<is>*.

Line 9 The sign rather like an Arabic 3, an example of abbreviation type 4(b), on this occasion stands for the omission of a final *'e'* in the word *dimiss<e>*, agreeing with *terr<e>*.

Line 14 Three examples of abbreviation type 2(d), *-rum,* the ending of the genitive plural, in this line.

Index

In addition to page reference to subjects and topics discussed in the introductory sections the index provides references to examples of some of the more difficult words, phrases, abbreviations and grammatical usages in the Latin extracts.